THE COMPLEAT ANGLER

Izaak Walton (1593–1683) is best known as the author of *The Compleat Angler* but he was also one of the earliest English biographers. Although of relatively humble birth he possessed a genius for friendship and was on close terms with many of the most eminent literary and ecclesiastical figures of his day. In politics he was a staunch Royalist (*The Compleat Angler* is in part a veiled satire against Puritans) and at the outset of the Civil War he retired from the successful city business he had built up and devoted the rest of his long life to literary studies.

Bryan Loughrey is Lecturer in English at the Roehampton Institute and a general editor, with Stephen Coote, of Penguin Masterstudies. He has contributed essays on Renaissance literature to a number of scholarly journals and has edited *The Pastoral Mode* for the Macmillan Casebook series.

IZAAK WALTON

THE COMPLEAT ANGLER

EDITED BY
BRYAN LOUGHREY

WITH A POSTSCRIPT BY
LORD HOME

PENGUIN BOOKS

Penguin Books Ltd, Harmondsworth, Middlesex, England
Viking Penguin Inc., 40 West 23rd Street, New York, New York 10010, U.S.A.
Penguin Books Australia Ltd, Ringwood, Victoria, Australia
Penguin Books Canada Ltd, 2801 John Street, Markham, Ontario, Canada L3R 1B4
Penguin Books (N.Z.) Ltd, 182–190 Wairau Road, Auckland 10, New Zealand

First published 1653
Published in Penguin Books 1985

Introduction and notes copyright © Bryan Loughrey, 1985
Postscript © Baron Home of the Hirsel, 1985
All rights reserved

Made and printed in Great Britain by
Richard Clay (The Chaucer Press) Ltd,
Bungay, Suffolk
Filmset in Monophoto Baskerville by Northumberland Press Ltd,
Gateshead, Tyne and Wear

Except in the United States of America,
this book is sold subject to the condition
that it shall not, by way of trade or otherwise,
be lent, re-sold, hired out, or otherwise circulated
without the publisher's prior consent in any form of
binding or cover other than that in which it is
published and without a similar condition
including this condition being imposed
on the subsequent purchaser

EDITOR'S INTRODUCTION

Izaak Walton was baptized[1] at St Mary's, Stafford, on 21 September 1593. His father, Gervase Walton, who had been described some years earlier as a 'tippler' or inn-keeper, died when the boy was five. His mother Anne subsequently remarried, again to a publican. These, unfortunately, are almost the only facts ascertainable concerning Walton's childhood and adolescence. It is tempting to assume that someone of his temperament and abilities would have attended the local Grammar School, but the scant evidence available suggests his formal education was limited.

What is certain, however, is that on 12 November 1618 Izaak Walton was admitted to the ranks of the Worshipful Company of Ironmongers. He must have made his way to London some years earlier and joined the household of his sister Anne, for the records indicate that he was apprenticed to her husband, Thomas Grinsell, a prosperous City linen-draper. Despite his membership of the Ironmongers' Company Walton probably also traded as a draper and sempster once he had completed his term of indenture. His business clearly flourished and in the years before the Civil War he held a number of important civic offices and purchased properties in both London and Stafford. He was not so fortunate in his family life. In 1626 he married Rachel Floud, a great-great-grandniece of Archbishop Cranmer. She died in 1640 having given birth to seven children, none of whom survived infancy.

In 1613 a poem by an unidentified 'S.P.', *The Love of Amos and Laura*, was published with dedicatory verses addressed 'To My Approved and Much Respected Friend, Iz. Wa.', indicating Walton had moved in literary circles from an early date. He was probably indebted to John Donne, however, for many of his extraordinarily diverse literary and ecclesiastic connections. Donne was appointed vicar of St Dunstan-in-the-West in 1624 and would have met

Walton, a vestryman and prominent resident, in the course of parish business. Although it is impossible to establish the exact nature of the relationship which developed, it must have been to some degree intimate. During the course of Donne's final illness Walton received from him a mourning ring bearing his personal seal and, according to their mutual friend Bishop Henry King,[2] Walton was among the privileged few permitted to visit Donne's death bed.

Walton's earliest surviving literary efforts are homages to the memory of Donne. He contributed an elegy to the 1633 first edition of Donne's poems, and lines by him subscribe the poet's portrait in the second edition. Donne was also the subject of the first of his great biographical essays. He came to write this almost by chance, for the project was originally proposed by Sir Henry Wotton and Walton was to have acted merely as a research assistant. Wotton's desultory efforts, however, were cut short by his death in 1639 and Walton was left to compose his *Life of Donne* in haste so that the edition of Donne's sermons should not appear before the public in 1640 'and want the *Authors Life*'.[3]

Walton thus became one of the earliest English biographers and would probably have expected, if he gave the subject any thought, that his literary reputation would be based on his *Lives* (of John Donne (1640); Henry Wotton (1651); Richard Hooker (1665); George Herbert (1670); and Robert Sanderson (1678)) rather than *The Compleat Angler*. He took pains to research his subjects thoroughly and, unusually for the period, documented the sources of his information. The aim of each *Life*, however, was to provide a harmonious portrait of the individual in the light of their Christian commitment. In Donne's case, for example, the early life of the poet is firmly subordinated to that of the Dean of St Paul's, which is delineated with impassioned eloquence:

> He was earnest and unwearied in the search of knowledge; with which his vigorous soul is now satisfied, and employed in a continual praise of that God that first breathed it into his active body; that body which once was a Temple of the Holy Ghost, and is now become a small quantity of Christian dust: But I shall see it reanimated.[4]

Walton retired from business in the early 1640s. It may be that he simply felt prosperous enough to concentrate on his studies and literary activities, but in all probability his decision was influenced by the outbreak of the Civil War. He was a staunch Royalist who would have found it difficult to continue to trade in the Republican stronghold of the City, particularly after the entry of the Scottish Convenanters in March 1643: 'This I saw and suffer'd by it.'[5] His first biographer, Antony à Wood, believed he remained in London until 'about 1643 (at which time he found it dangerous for honest men to be there,) he left that city, and lived sometimes at Stafford, and elsewhere, but mostly in the families of the eminent clergymen of England, of whom he was much beloved'.[6] If this is so, he must have visited London frequently, for he married his second wife, Anne Ken, at Clerkenwell Church in 1646 and appears to have resided in that parish at least intermittently until 1660. He was certainly in London at the time of Archbishop Laud's execution in January 1645 and recorded that event with incredulous horror:

> And about this time the Bishop of *Canterbury* having been by an unknown Law condemned to die, and the execution suspended for some days, many of the malicious Citizens fearing his pardon, shut up their Shops, professing not to open them till Justice was executed. This malice and madness is scarce credible, but I saw it.[7]

Walton wrote this after the Restoration, but he had been an outspoken critic of the revolutionary regime even when it held power. His *Life of Wotton*, for example, published only two years after the execution of Charles I, boldly catalogued the pernicious effects of the '*Church Militant*' upon the Nation:

> where the weeds of controversie grow to be daily more numerous, and more destructive to humble Piety; and where men have Consciences that boggle at Ceremonies, and yet scruple not to speak and act such sins as the ancient humble Christians believed to be a sinne to think; where (as our Revered *Hooker* sayes) *Former Simplicity and softness of spirit, is not now to be found, because Zeal hath drowned Charity, and skill meekness* ...[8]

The Compleat Angler, first published in 1653, needs to be read in this context. Angling was a pursuit associated with the sequestered Anglican clergy,[9] and the celebration of 'all that love *Vertue* and *Angling*'[10] and satire against (probably Puritan) 'men of sowre complexions; money-getting-men'[11] therefore had topical relevance.

Walton's loyalty to the Crown was sufficiently well known for him to be entrusted, after the final defeat of the Royalist forces at the Battle of Worcester, with the safe conveyance of a royal jewel known as the Lesser George.

The restoration of the monarchy (welcomed by Walton in a joyous pastoral eclogue, 'Damon and Dorus') and episcopacy brought Walton's ecclesiastic friends to positions of influence, and they were quick to reciprocate the acts of goodwill he had displayed towards them during the Interregnum. In particular, his old friend George Morley, now Bishop of Worcester, provided him with a home and employment in the probably nominal position of personal steward. In 1662 his wife died and was buried at Worcester Cathedral with an epitaph composed by her husband. Later that year Walton accompanied Morley to Winchester and took up residence with his two children at Farnham Castle. He made full use of Morley's hospitality, bringing out his *Life of Hooker* (which was commissioned by the Archbishop of Canterbury, Gilbert Sheldon, and based on information provided by his Cranmer relations) in 1665 and his *Life of Herbert* in 1670.

After the marriage of his daughter Anne to Dr William Hawkins, a Prebendary of Winchester Cathedral, Walton spent much of his time in their home at Droxford. His son Isaac was tutored by Thomas Ken (who was the younger half-brother of his second wife and was later appointed Bishop of Bath and Wells) and after studying at Oxford became a Canon of Salisbury Cathedral. Walton remained active in his old age. His visits to his many friends were frequent and often extended. He made, for example, the strenuous journey to the Peak District to fish the river Dove with Charles Cotton, the author of the supplement on fly-fishing published as the second part of *The Compleat Angler* in 1676. Nor did Walton abate his literary efforts. He continually revised his published works and in 1676 brought out his *Life of Sanderson*, another eminent clergyman with whom he was personally acquainted. In the final year of his life he edited *Thealma and Clearchus*, a poem by John Chalkhill, a relative of his second wife.

Walton died in his daughter's home on 15 December 1683 and was buried in Winchester Cathedral.

THE WORK

The Compleat Angler is both a manual of instruction and a prose idyll. It is therefore best considered within the traditions of georgic and pastoral.[12]

The view that poetry is primarily concerned with the expression of personal emotion is a relatively modern prejudice. Before the triumph of scientific rationalism effectively divorced the arts and sciences, poetry was thought of as a natural medium of instruction and didactic verse or georgic was a highly regarded form. The genre originated with Hesiod's *Works and Days* (*c.* eighth century B.C.), but the most influential model was Virgil's *Georgics* (*c.* 30 B.C.), a long poem on and in praise of husbandry. Its four books describe the keeping of crops, trees, cattle and bees, associating these activities with a distinctive moral vision. Agriculture is seen as 'the embodiment of permanence and as a foundation of peace and prosperity'.[13] The simple farmer, whose life is governed by the rhythms of nature and the traditional pieties, is held up as a morally superior being, untainted by the vicious propensities of urban existence. Rural tranquillity is also contrasted with the horrors of war and as a result Virgil (who like Walton wrote in a time of civil strife) is able to incorporate political propaganda in support of Octavius Caesar, the only leader he regarded as capable of establishing the strong central authority which alone could guarantee peace.

Georgics on other rural occupations, including hunting and fishing, were written in imitation of Virgil and generally retained his note of quietism. The medieval and Renaissance vernacular texts on horticulture and the field sports also tended towards moralities. The earliest English piscatory, for example, Dame Juliana Berners's *Treatyse of Fysshynge with an Angle* (1496), not only provides information on fish and fishing, but lays great stress on the moral qualities the angler needs to possess. Walton certainly knew this work, either in the original or through Leonard Mascall's *Booke of Fishing with Hooke and Line* (1590), as well as a number of other early texts on angling which married practical with ethical instruction. They probably influenced both the pious temper of *The Compleat Angler* and its structure. William Samuel's *Arte of Angling* (1577) is particularly interesting in this context, for it shares many features with the *Angler*, including the format of a dialogue between an experienced angler named *Piscator* and his pupil *Viator*.

The Compleat Angler obviously displays many georgic traits. It provides detailed instruction in a rural pursuit; depicts the tranquil pleasures of the countryside; and celebrates the moral superiority of those 'that hate contentions, and love *quietnesse*, and *vertue*, and *Angling*'.[14] Despite the fact that it is written in prose it even shares some formal characteristics with georgic verse. Piscator opens his discourse, for example, with the traditional mythological account of the antiquity and origins of the art, although significantly he is careful to provide angling with a biblical as well as a classical ancestry.

Certain features of *The Compleat Angler*, however, can only be appreciated within the context of the pastoral tradition. Both georgic and pastoral contrast the town and the country to the advantage of the latter: 'God made the country, and man made the town.'[15] But they differ sharply in their attitude to the natural world. Georgic celebrates the fertility of the fields and the dignity of productive labour. Pastoral, on the other hand, depicts an idealized version of the countryside and proclaims the prerogatives of leisure and love.[16] Virgil again supplied the most influential paradigm and the *Eclogues* (*c.* 39 B.C.) firmly established the simple shepherd as the typical representative of pastoral innocence and the stylized landscape of Arcadia as his natural environment. Walton would also have been aware, however, of a minor tradition of pastoral, stemming from the example of Sannazaro's *Piscatoria* (1526), in which fishermen replaced shepherds as spokesmen for pastoral values.

Although *The Compleat Angler* does not employ the shepherd of literary convention, it retains many of the features of formal pastoral. The Lea valley, for example, despite the presence of contemporary landmarks is described in Arcadian rather than naturalistic terms:

Look, under that broad *Beech tree* I sate down when I was last this way a fishing, and the birds in the adjoining Grove seemed to have a friendly contention with an Echo, whose dead voice seemed to live in a hollow cave, near to the brow of that Primrose hil; there I sate viewing the Silver streams glide silently towards their center, the tempestuous Sea, yet sometimes opposed by rugged roots, and pibble stones, which broke their waves, and turned them into fome: and sometimes viewing the harmless Lambs, some leaping securely in the cool shade, whilst others sported themselvs in the cheerful Sun; and others were craving comfort from the swolne Udders of their bleating Dams. As I thus sate, these and other signs had so fully possest my soul, that I thought as the Poet has happily exprest it:

> *I was for that time lifted above earth;*
> *And possest joyes not promis'd in my birth.*

As I left this place, and entered into the next field, a second pleasure entertained me, 'twas a handsome Milk-maid, that had cast away all care, and sung like a *Nightingale*; her voice was good, and the Ditty fitted for it; 'twas that smooth Song which was made by *Kit Marlow*, now at least fifty years ago; and the Milkmaids mother sung an answer to it, which was made by Sir *Walter Raleigh* in his yonger dayes.[17]

This passage consciously introduces classical allusions into the English landscape. Virgil's 'Eclogue I', to which *Piscator* later refers,[18] is the source of the 'broad *Beech tree*'. The curious Echo, 'whose dead voice seemed to live in a hollow cave', insinuates Ovid's metamorphosed nymph into the scene. Harmless lambs recall the shepherd's trade and it comes as no surprise to learn that the 'handsome Milk-maid' passes the time singing pastoral lyrics.

The value-structure of the *Angler* is also consistently pastoral in spirit. The countryside is celebrated as a source of spiritual refreshment, and the vexations of 'money-getting-men ... that are condemn'd to be rich, and alwayes discontented, or busie'[19] are contrasted with the carefree existence of anglers. Viator's admission to that fraternity is dependent not only on the acquisition of a set of skills, but on absorbing an entire philosophy of life. Thus a resolution of georgic and pastoral values is achieved through the special status of angling. It is an activity which demands a particular expertise. But it is also a leisure pursuit which encourages introspection. 'Action' and 'Contemplation' thus 'meet together, and do most properly belong to the most honest, ingenious, harmless Art of Angling'.[20]

THE TEXT

Walton revised *The Compleat Angler* over a period of twenty-three years, and the four editions which he supervised through the press are sufficiently distinct to warrant individual notice.

The 1653 first edition is a relatively slim volume of thirteen chapters which intersperses practical instruction with pastoral interludes and introduces the basic dramatic structure to which all later editions adhere. It was published by Walton's friend Richard Marriot and sold from his shop in St Dunstan's churchyard.

The second edition of 1655 contains twenty-one chapters and is almost half as long again as the first edition. It was expanded in a number of ways. A third interlocutor, *Auceps*, is introduced and takes part in a debate on the respective merits of hawking, hunting and angling. Some extra songs supplement the 'innocent Mirth', and Walton also extended some sections of pious reflection. But the vast bulk of the additional material consists of practical information on the natural history of fishes, often borrowed directly from other works, aimed at making the *Angler* a more comprehensive manual.

The third edition appeared in 1661, and the restoration of the monarchy in the previous year occasioned a number of minor changes. The majority of the alterations, however, are introduced to heighten the literary effect and dignify the subject material. Walton also introduced an elegiac note into the work. The Preface to the earlier two editions had stated that 'the whole discourse is a kind of picture of my own disposition in such dayes and times, as I allow to my self, when honest *Nat.* and *R.R.* and I go a fishing together'. In the third edition this reads: '*the whole Discourse is, or rather was, a picture of my own disposition, especially in such dayes and times as I have laid aside business, and gone a fishing with honest* Nat. *and* R. Roe; *but they are gone, and with them most of my pleasant hours, even as a shadow that passeth away, and returnes not.*'[21] The fourth edition of 1668 is virtually a reprint of the third and probably did not receive Walton's personal supervision.

The fifth edition was brought out in 1676 with a supplement on fly-fishing and Robert Venable's *Experienc'd Angler*, the three works bound together and entitled *The Universal Angler*. Walton had again carefully revised his text, adding little in the way of practical information on fishing, but enhancing the encyclopaedic nature of the work through the addition of numerous citations from scholarly authorities. He also further reinforced its pious tone, adding to the last chapter, for example, a lengthy sermon on the virtues of humility and gratitude.

Most editors have followed the text of the fifth edition, the last to appear in Walton's lifetime. The text reproduced here, however, is that of the 1653 first edition. As I have tried to show above, each edition has a distinct character and can be read in its own right. The first edition is a work of considerable merit which has not been readily available, so the decision to reprint is not, I hope, entirely eccentric. There are inevitable losses, such as the enforced omission of Auceps' magnificent paean to the nightingale, which first appeared in 1655:

But the Nightingale (another of my Airy Creatures) breaths such sweet loud musick out of her little instrumental throat, that it might make mankind to think Miracles are not ceased. He that at midnight (when the very labourer sleeps securely) should hear (as I have very often) the clear airs, the sweet descants, the natural rising and falling, the doubling and redoubling of her voice, might well be lifted above earth, and say; Lord, what Musick has thou provided for the Saints in Heaven, when thou affordest bad men such musick on Earth![22]

There are, however, compensations. Sir Nicholas Harris Nicholas thought some of the alterations to the fifth edition betrayed 'the garrulity and sentiments of an octogenarian'[23] and it is not always clear that Walton's revisions constitute improvements. Moreover, the 1653 edition preserves a fine sense of proportion. In particular, the dramatic structure, which at times is almost overwhelmed by a wealth of fabulous love and pious moralizing in later editions, remains clearly evident and provides a satisfactory framework for the heterogeneous elements of *The Compleat Angler*.

My editorial procedure has been conservative. I have retained the eccentric and often inconsistent spelling of the original (which prints, for example, *Compleat* in the title but *Complete* in the page headings), but modernized 'ʃ' to 's' and 'vv' to 'w'. Square brackets have been omitted where they open but do not close quotations or where they merely accompany quotations in the margin. In all other cases square brackets have been standardized to round brackets. The footnotes from the original, marked by asterisks, have been retained, but the original side-notes have been keyed to the text with daggers and removed to the foot of the page. The editor's notes are not keyed to the text but are arranged by page number at the end of the book. A few obvious misprints have been corrected; superscripts have been written out in full and speech prefixes regularized. The illustrations are taken from the first edition but in some cases have had to be moved slightly from their original positions.

The Compleat Angler or the Contemplative man's Recreation.

Being a Discourse of

FISH and FISHING,

Not unworthy the perusal of most *Anglers*.

Simon Peter *said, I go a* fishing : *and they said, We
also will go with thee.* John 21.3. May. 20.

London, Printed by T. Maxey for RICH. MARRIOT, in
S. Dunstans Church-yard Fleetstreet, 1653.

JOHN OFFLEY

Of MADELY Manor in the
County of *Stafford*, Esq;
My most honoured Friend.   5

SIR,

I *Have made so ill use of your former favors, as by them to be encouraged to
intreat that they may be enlarged to the* patronage *and* protection *of this
Book; and I have put on a modest confidence, that I shall not be denyed,
because 'tis a discourse of* Fish *and* Fishing, *which you both know so well,* 10
and love and practice so much.

   You are assur'd (though there be ignorant men of an other belief) that
Angling *is an Art; and you know that Art better then any that I know:
and that this is truth, is demonstrated by the fruits of that pleasant labor
which you enjoy when you purpose to give rest to your mind, and devest your* 15
*self of your more serious business, and (which is often) dedicate a day or
two to this* Recreation.

   *At which time, if common Anglers should attend you, and be eye-
witnesses of the success, not of your fortune, but your skill, it would doubtless
beget in them an emulation to be like you, and that emulation might beget* 20
*an industrious diligence to be so: but I know it is not atainable by common
capacities.*

   *Sir, this pleasant curiositie of Fish and Fishing (of which you are so great
a Master) has been thought worthy the* pens *and* practices *of divers in other
Nations, which have been reputed men of great Learning *and* Wisdome; 25
and amongst those of this Nation, I remember Sir Henry Wotton *(a dear
lover of this Art) has told me, that his intentions were to write a discourse
of the Art, and in the praise of* Angling, *and doubtless he had done so,
if death had not prevented him; the remembrance of which hath often made
me sorry; for, if he had lived to do it, then the unlearned* Angler *(of which* 30
*I am one) had seen some Treatise of this Art worthy his perusal which
(though some have undertaken it) I could never yet see in English.*

But mine may be thought as weak *and as* unworthy *of common view: and I do here freely confess, that I should rather excuse my self, then censure others, my own Discourse being liable to so many exceptions; against which, you (Sir) might make this one,* That it can contribute nothing to your
5 knowledge; *and lest a longer Epistle may diminish your pleasure, I shal not adventure to make this Epistle longer then to add this following truth,*
That I am really, Sir,
Your most affectionate Friend,
and most humble Servant,
Iz. Wa.

TO THE
Reader of this Discourse:
But especially,
To the honest ANGLER.

I Think fit to tell thee these following truths; that I did not undertake 5
to write, or to publish this discourse of *fish* and *fishing*, to please
my self, and that I wish it may not displease others; for, I have
confest there are many defects in it. And yet, I cannot doubt, but
that by it, some readers may receive so much *profit* or *pleasure*, as
if they be not very busie men, may make it not unworthy the time 10
of their perusall; and this is all the confidence that I can put on
concerning the merit of this Book.

And I wish the Reader also to take notice, that in writing of
it, I have made a recreation, of a recreation; and that it might
prove so to thee in the reading, and not to read *dull*, and *tediously*, 15
I have in severall places mixt some innocent Mirth; of which, if
thou be a severe, sowr complexioned man, then I here disallow
thee to be a competent Judg. For Divines say, *there are offences*
given; and *offences taken, but not given*. And I am the willinger to justifie
this *innocent Mirth*, because the whole discourse is a kind of picture 20
of my owne disposition, at least of my disposition in such daies and
times as I allow my self, when honest *Nat.* and *R.R.* and I go a
fishing together; and let me adde this, that he that likes not the
discourse, should like the pictures of the *Trout* and other fish, which
I may commend, because they concern not my self. 25

And I am also to tel the Reader, that in that which is the more
usefull part of this discourse, that is to say, the observations of the
nature and *breeding*, and *seasons*, and *catching of fish*, I am not so simple
as to think but that he may find exceptions in some of these; and
therefore I must intreat him to know, or rather note, that severall 30
Countreys, and several Rivers alter the *time* and *manner* of fishes

Breeding; and therefore if he bring not candor to the reading of
this Discourse, he shall both injure me, and possibly himself too
by too many Criticisms.

Now for the Art of catching fish; that is to say, how to make
5 a man that was none, an Angler by a book: he that undertakes it,
shall undertake a harder task then *Hales*, that in his printed Book*
undertook by it to teach the Art of Fencing, and was laught at
for his labour. Not but that something usefull might be observed
out of that Book; but that Art was not to be taught by words; nor
10 is the Art of Angling. And yet, I think, that most that love that
Game, may here learn something that may be worth their money,
if they be not needy: and if they be, then my advise is, that they
forbear; for, I write not to get money, but for pleasure; and this
discourse boasts of no more: for I hate to promise much, and fail.

15 But pleasure I have found both in the *search* and *conference* about
what is here offered to thy view and censure; I wish thee as much
in the perusal of it, and so might here take my leave; but I will
stay thee a little longer by telling thee, that whereas it is said by
many, that in *Fly-fishing* for a *Trout*, the Angler must observe his
20 twelve Flyes for every Month; I say, if he observe that, he shall
be as certain to catch fish, as they that make Hay by the fair dayes
in Almanacks, and be no surer: for doubtless, three or four *Flyes*
rightly made, do serve for a *Trout* all *Summer*; and for *Winter-flies*,
all *Anglers* know, they are as useful as an *Almanack* out of date.

25 Of these (because no man is born an *Artist* nor an *Angler*) I thought
fit to give thee this notice. I might say more, but it is not fit for
this place; but if this Discourse which follows shall come to a second
impression, which is possible, for slight books have been in this Age
observed to have that fortune; I shall then for thy sake be glad
30 to correct what is faulty, or by a conference with any to explain
or enlarge what is defective: but for this time I have neither a
willingness nor leasure to say more, then wish thee a *rainy evening*
to read this book in, and *that the east wind may never blow when thou
goest a fishing*. Farewel.

35   IZ. WA.

* Called the private School of defence.

Because in this Discourse of *Fish* and *Fishing* I have not observed a method, which (though the Discourse be not long) may be some inconvenience to the Reader, I have therefore for his easier finding out some particular things which are spoken of, made this following Table. 5

These directions the Reader may take as an ease in his search after some particular Fish, and the baits proper for them; and he will shew himselfe courteous in mending or passing by some few errors in the Printer, which are not so many but that they may be pardoned.

The Complete
ANGLER

OR,
The contemplative Mans
RECREATION.

5

$$\left\{ \begin{array}{c} \text{PISCATOR.} \\ \text{VIATOR.} \end{array} \right\}$$

Piscator. You are wel overtaken Sir; a good morning to you; I have stretch'd my legs up *Totnam Hil* to overtake you, hoping your businesse may occasion you towards *Ware*, this fine pleasant 10 fresh *May day* in the Morning.

Viator. Sir, I shall almost answer your hopes: for my purpose is to be at *Hodsden* (three miles short of that Town) I will not say, before I drink; but before I break my fast: for I have appointed a friend or two to meet me there at the *thatcht house*, about nine 15 of the clock this morning; and that made me so early up, and indeed, to walk so fast.

Pisc. Sir, I know the *thatcht house* very well: I often make it my resting place, and taste a cup of Ale there, for which liquor that place is very remarkable; and to that house I shall by your favour 20 accompany you, and either abate of my pace, or mend it, to enjoy such a companion as you seem to be, knowing that (as the Italians say) *Good company makes the way seem the shorter*.

Viat. It may do so Sir, with the help of good discourse, which (methinks) I may promise from you, that both look and speak so 25 chearfully. And to invite you to it, I do here promise you, that for my part, I will be as free and open-hearted, as discretion will warrant me to be with a stranger.

Pisc. Sir, I am right glad of your answer; and in confidence that you speak the truth, I shall (Sir) put on a boldnesse to ask, whether 30 pleasure or businesse hath occasioned your Journey.

3

Viat. Indeed, Sir, a little businesse, and more pleasure: for my purpose is to bestow a day or two in hunting the *Otter* (which my friend that I go to meet, tells me is more pleasant then any hunting whatsoever:) and having dispatcht a little businesse this
5 day, my purpose is to morrow to follow a pack of dogs of honest Mr——, who hath appointed me and my friend to meet him upon *Amwel hill* to morrow morning by day break.

Pisc. Sir, my fortune hath answered my desires; and my purpose is to bestow a day or two in helping to destroy some of those
10 villanous vermin: for I hate them perfectly, because they love fish so well, or rather, because they destroy so much: indeed, so much, that in my judgment, all men that keep Otter dogs ought to have a Pension from the Commonwealth to incourage them to destroy the very breed of those base *Otters*, they do so much mischief.

15 *Viat.* But what say you to the *Foxes* of this Nation? would not you as willingly have them destroyed? for doubtlesse they do as much mischief as the *Otters* do.

Pisc. Oh Sir, if they do, it is not so much to me and my Fraternitie, as that base Vermin the *Otters* do.

20 *Viat.* Why Sir, I pray, of what Fraternity are you, that you are so angry with the poor *Otter*?

Pisc. I am a Brother of the *Angle*, and therefore an enemy to the *Otter*, he does me and my friends so much mischief; for you are to know, that we *Anglers* all love one another: and therefore do I
25 hate the *Otter* perfectly, even for their sakes that are of my Brotherhood.

Viat. Sir, to be plain with you, I am sorry you are an *Angler*: for I have heard many grave, serious men pitie, and many pleasant men scoffe at *Anglers*.

30 *Pisc.* Sir, There are many men that are by others taken to be serious grave men, which we contemn and pitie; men of sowre complexions; money-getting-men, that spend all their time first in getting, and next in anxious care to keep it: men that are condemn'd to be rich, and alwayes discontented, or busie. For these
35 poor-rich-men, wee Anglers pitie them; and stand in no need to borrow their thoughts to think our selves happie: For (trust me, Sir) we enjoy a contentednesse above the reach of such dispositions.

And as for any scoffer, *qui mockat mockabitur*. Let mee tell you, (that you may tell him) what the wittie French-man sayes in such a Case. *When my* Cat *and I entertaine each other with mutuall apish tricks* †
(as playing with a garter,) who knows but that I make her more sport then she makes me? Shall I conclude her simple, that has her time to begin or 5
refuse sportivenesse as freely as I my self have? Nay, who knows but that our agreeing no better, is the defect of my not understanding her language? (for doubtlesse Cats talk and reason with one another) and that shee laughs at, and censures my folly, for making her sport, and pities mee for under-standing her no better? To this purpose speaks *Mountagne* concerning 10
Cats: And I hope I may take as great a libertie to blame any Scoffer, that has never heard what an Angler can say in the justification of his Art and Pleasure.

But, if this satisfie not, I pray bid the Scoffer put this Epigram into his pocket, and read it every morning for his breakfast (for 15
I wish him no better;) Hee shall finde it fix'd before the Dialogues of *Lucian* (who may be justly accounted the father of the Family of all *Scoffers*:) And though I owe none of that Fraternitie so much as good will, yet I have taken a little pleasant pains to make such a conversion of it as may make it the fitter for all of that Fraternity. 20

> Lucian *well skill'd in* scoffing, *this has writ.*
> *Friend, that's your folly which you think your wit:*
> *This you vent oft, void both of* wit *and* fear,
> *Meaning an other, when your self you jeer.*

But no more of the *Scoffer*; for since *Solomon* sayes, he is an 25
abomination to men, he shall be so to me; and I think, to all that ⸸
love *Vertue* and *Angling*.

Viat. Sir, you have almost amazed me: for though I am no Scoffer, yet I have (I pray let me speak it without offence) always look'd upon *Anglers* as more patient, and more simple men, then (I fear) 30
I shall finde you to be.

Pisc. Sir, I hope you will not judge my earnestnesse to be impatience: and for my *simplicitie*, if by that you mean a *harmlesnesse*, or that *simplicity* that was usually found in the Primitive Christians,

† The Lord Mountagne in his Apol. for Ra. Sebond.
⸸ Pro. 24.9.

who were (as most *Anglers* are) quiet men, and followed peace; men
that were too wise to sell their consciences to buy riches for vexation,
and a fear to die; men that lived in those times when there were
fewer Lawyers; for then a Lordship might have been safely conveyed
5 in a piece of Parchment no bigger then your hand, though several
skins are not sufficient to do it in this wiser Age. I say, Sir, if you
take us Anglers to be such simple men as I have spoken of, then
both my self, and those of my profession will be glad to be so
understood. But if by simplicitie you meant to expresse any general
10 defect in the understanding of those that professe and practice
Angling, I hope to make it appear to you, that there is so much
contrary reason (if you have but the patience to hear it) as may
remove all the anticipations that Time or Discourse may have
possess'd you with, against that Ancient and laudable Art.

15 *Viat.* Why (Sir) is Angling of Antiquitie, and an Art, and an
art not easily learn'd?

Pisc. Yes (Sir:) and I doubt not but that if you and I were to
converse together but til night, I should leave you possess'd with
the same happie thoughts that now possesse me; not onely for the
20 Antiquitie of it, but that it deserves commendations; and that 'tis
an Art; and worthy the knowledge and practice of a wise, and a
serious man.

Viat. Sir, I pray speak of them what you shall think fit; for wee
have yet five miles to walk before wee shall come to the
25 *Thatcht house.* And, Sir, though my infirmities are many, yet I dare
promise you, that both my patience and attention will indure to
hear what you will say till wee come thither: and if you please to
begin in order with the antiquity, when that is done, you shall not
want my attention to the commendations and accommodations of
30 it: and lastly, if you shall convince me that 'tis an Art, and an
Art worth learning, I shall beg I may become your Scholer, both
to wait upon you, and to be instructed in the Art it self.

Pisc. Oh Sir, 'tis not to be questioned, but that it is an art, and
an art worth your Learning: the question wil rather be, whether
35 you be capable of learning it? For he that learns it, must not only
bring an enquiring, searching, and discerning wit; but he must bring
also that *patience* you talk of, and a love and propensity to the art

it self: but having once got and practised it, then doubt not but the Art will (both for the pleasure and profit of it) prove like to *Vertue, a reward to it self.*

Viat. Sir, I am now become so ful of expectation, that I long much to have you proceed in your discourse: And first, I pray Sir, 5 let me hear concerning the antiquity of it.

Pisc. Sir, I wil preface no longer, but proceed in order as you desire me: And first for the Antiquity of *Angling*, I shall not say much; but onely this; Some say, it is as ancient as *Deucalions* Floud: †
and others (which I like better) say, that *Belus* (who was the inventer † 10
of godly and vertuous Recreations) was the Inventor of it: and some others say, (for former times have had their Disquisitions about it) that *Seth*, one of the Sons of *Adam*, taught it to his sons, and that by them it was derived to Posterity. Others say, that he left it engraven on those Pillars which hee erected to preserve the 15
knowledg of the *Mathematicks, Musick*, and the rest of those precious Arts, which by Gods appointment or allowance, and his noble industry were thereby preserved from perishing in *Noah's* Floud.

These (my worthy Friend) have been the opinions of some men, that possibly may have endeavoured to make it more ancient then 20
may well be warranted. But for my part, I shall content my self in telling you, That *Angling* is much more ancient then the incarnation of our Saviour: For both in the Prophet *Amos*, and ‡
before him in *Job*, (which last Book is judged to be written by ‡
Moses) mention is made of *fish-hooks*, which must imply *Anglers* in 25
those times.

But (my worthy friend) as I would rather prove my self to be a Gentleman, by being *learned* and *humble, valiant* and *inoffensive, vertuous* and *communicable*, then by a fond ostentation of *riches*; or (wanting these Vertues my self) boast that these were in my 30
Ancestors; (And yet I confesse, that where a noble and ancient Descent and such Merits meet in any man, it is a double dignifica- tion of that person:) and so, if this Antiquitie of Angling (which,

† J. Da.
† Jer. Mar.
‡ Chap. 4.2.
‡ Chap. 41.

for my part, I have not forc'd) shall, like an ancient Familie, be either an honour, or an ornament to this vertuous Art which I both love and practise, I shall be the gladder that I made an accidental mention of it; and shall proceed to the justification, or rather
5 commendation of it.

Viat. My worthy Friend, I am much pleased with your discourse, for that you seem to be so ingenuous, and so modest, as not to stretch arguments into Hyperbolicall expressions, but such as indeed they will reasonably bear; and I pray, proceed to the
10 justification, or commendations of Angling, which I also long to hear from you.

Pisc. Sir, I shall proceed; and my next discourse shall be rather a Commendation, then a Justification of Angling: for, in my judgment, if it deserves to be commended, it is more then justified; for
15 some practices that may be justified, deserve no commendation: yet there are none that deserve commendation but may be justified.

And now having said thus much by way of preparation, I am next to tell you, that in ancient times a debate hath risen, (and it is not yet resolved) Whether *Contemplation* or *Action* be the chiefest
20 thing wherin the happiness of a man doth most consist in this world?

Concerning which, some have maintained their opinion of the first, by saying, 'That the nearer we Mortals come to God by way of imitation, the more happy we are.' And that God injoyes himself only by *Contemplation* of his own *Goodness*, *Eternity*, *Infiniteness* and
25 *Power*, and the like; and upon this ground many of them prefer *Contemplation* before *Action*: and indeed, many of the Fathers seem to approve this opinion, as may appear in their Comments upon the words of our Saviour to * *Martha*.

And contrary to these, others of equal Authority and credit, have
30 preferred *Action* to be chief; as experiments in *Physick*, and the application of it, both for the ease and prolongation of man's life, by which man is enabled to act, and to do good to others: And they say also, That *Action* is not only Doctrinal, but a maintainer of humane Society; and for these, and other reasons, to be preferr'd
35 before *Contemplation*.

* Luk. 10.41, 42.

Concerning which two opinions, I shall forbear to add a third, by declaring my own, and rest my self contented in telling you (my worthy friend) that both these meet together, and do most properly belong to the most honest, ingenious, harmless Art of Angling.

And first I shall tel you what some have observed, and I have 5 found in my self, That the very sitting by the Rivers side, is not only the fittest place for, but will invite the Anglers to Contemplation: That it is the fittest place, seems to be witnessed by the children of *Israel**, who having banish'd all mirth and Musick from their pensive hearts, and having hung up their then mute 10 Instruments upon the Willow trees, growing by the Rivers of *Babylon*, sate down upon those banks bemoaning the *ruines* of *Sion*, and contemplating their own sad condition.

And an ingenuous *Spaniard* says, 'That both Rivers, and the inhabitants of the watery Element, were created for wise men to 15 contemplate, and fools to pass by without consideration.' And though I am too wise to rank my self in the first number, yet give me leave to free my self from the last, by offering to thee a short contemplation, first of Rivers, and then of Fish: concerning which, I doubt not but to relate to you many things very considerable. 20

Concerning Rivers, there be divers wonders reported of them by Authors, of such credit, that we need not deny them an Historical faith.

As of a River in *Epirus*, that puts out any lighted Torch, and kindles any Torch that was not lighted. Of the River *Selarus*, that 25 in a few hours turns a rod or a wand into stone (and our *Camden* mentions the like wonders in *England*:) that there is a river in *Arabia*, of which all the Sheep that drink thereof have their Wool turned into a Vermilion colour. And one of no less credit then *Aristotle*, tels us of a merry River, the River *Elusina*, that dances † 3 at the noise of Musick, that with Musick it bubbles, dances, and growes sandy, but returns to a wonted calmness and clearness when the Musick ceases. And lastly, (for I would not tire your patience) *Josephus*, that learned *Jew*, tells us of a River in *Judea*, that runs and moves swiftly all the six dayes of the week, and stands still and 35

* Psal. 137.
† In his *Wonders of nature*. This is confirmed by *Ennius* and *Solon* in his holy History.

rests upon their *Sabbath* day. But Sir, lest this discourse may seem tedious, I shall give it a sweet conclusion out of the holy Poet Mr *George Herbert* his Divine Contemplation on Gods providence.

> *Lord, who hath praise enough, nay, who hath any?*
> 5 *None can express thy works, but he that knows them;*
> *And none can know thy works, they are so many,*
> *And so complete, but only he that owes them.*
>
> *We all acknowledge both thy power and love*
> *To be exact, transcendent, and divine;*
> 10 *Who dost so strangely, and so sweetly move,*
> *Whilst all things have their end, yet none but thine.*
>
> *Wherefore, most Sacred Spirit, I here present*
> *For me, and all my fellows, praise to thee;*
> *And just it is that I should pay the rent,*
> 15 *Because the benefit accrues to me.*

† And as concerning Fish, in that Psalm, wherein for height of Poetry and Wonders, the Prophet *David* seems even to exceed himself; how doth he there express himselfe in choice Metaphors, even to the amazement of a contemplative Reader, concerning the Sea, 20 the Rivers, and the Fish therein contained. And the great Naturallist *Pliny* says, 'That Natures great and wonderful power is more demonstrated in the Sea, then on the Land.' And this may appear by the numerous and various Creatures, inhabiting both in and about that Element: as to the Readers of *Gesner, Randelitius, Pliny,* 25 *Aristotle,* and others is demonstrated: But I will sweeten this dis-
† course also out of a contemplation in Divine *Dubartas,* who says,

> *God quickned in the Sea and in the rivers,*
> *So many fishes of so many features,*
> *That in the waters we may see all Creatures;*
> 30 *Even all that on the earth is to be found,*
> *As if the world were in deep waters drownd.*
> *For seas (as well as Skies) have Sun, Moon, Stars;*
> *(As wel as air) Swallows, Rooks, and Stares;*
> *(As wel as earth) Vines, Roses, Nettles, Melons,*

† Psal. 104.
† Dubartas in the fifth day.

Mushroms, Pinks, Gilliflowers and many milions
Of other plants, more rare, more strange then these;
As very fishes living in the seas;
And also Rams, Calves, Horses, Hares and Hogs,
Wolves, Urchins, Lions, Elephants and Dogs;   5
Yea, Men and Maids, and which I most admire,
The Mitred Bishop, and the cowled Fryer.
Of which examples but a few years since,
Were shewn the Norway *and* Polonian *Prince.*

These seem to be wonders, but have had so many confirmations   10
from men of Learning and credit, that you need not doubt them;
nor are the number, nor the various shapes of fishes, more strange
or more fit for *contemplation*, then their different natures, inclinations
and actions: concerning which I shall beg your patient ear a little
longer.   15

The *Cuttle-fish* will cast a long gut out of her throat, which (like
as an Angler does his line) she sendeth forth and pulleth in again
at her pleasure, according as she sees some little fish come neer
to her; and the *Cuttle-fish* (being then hid in the gravel) lets the
smaller fish nibble and bite the end of it; at which time shee by   20
little and little draws the smaller fish so neer to her, that she may
leap upon her, and then catches and devours her: and for this reason   †
some have called this fish the *Sea-Angler*.

There are also lustful and chaste fishes, of which I shall also give
you examples.   25

And first, what *Dubartas* sayes of a fish called the *Sargus*; which
(because none can express it better then he does) I shall give you
in his own words, supposing it shall not have the less credit for being
Verse, for he hath gathered this, and other observations out of
Authors that have been great and industrious searchers into the   30
secrets of nature.

> *The Adulterous* Sargus *doth not only change,*
> *Wives everyday in the deep streams, but (strange)*
> *As if the honey of Sea-love delight*
> *Could not suffice his ranging appetite,*   35

† *Mount. Essayes*: and others affirm this.

31

> *Goes courting* She-Goats *on the grassie shore,*
> *Horning their husbands that had horns before.*

And the same Author writes concerning the *Cantharus*, that which
you shall also heare in his own words.

5
> *But contrary, the constant* Cantharus,
> *Is ever constant to his faithful Spouse,*
> *In nuptial duties spending his chaste life,*
> *Never loves any but his own dear wife.*

Sir, but a little longer, and I have done.

10 *Viat.* Sir, take what liberty you think fit, for your discourse seems
to be Musick, and charms me into an attention.

Pisc. Why then Sir, I will take a little libertie to tell, or rather
to remember you what is said of *Turtle Doves*: First, that they silently
plight their troth and marry; and that then, the Survivor scorns
15 (as the *Thracian* women are said to do) to outlive his or her Mate;
and this is taken for such a truth, that if the Survivor shall ever
couple with another, the he or she, not only the living, but the
dead, is denyed the *name* and *honour* of a true *Turtle Dove*.

And to parallel this Land Rarity, and teach mankind moral faith-
20 fulness, and to condemn those that talk of Religion, and yet come
short of the moral faith of fish and fowl; Men that violate the Law,
† affirm'd by Saint *Paul* to be writ in their hearts, and which he sayes
shal at the last day condemn and leave them without excuse, I Pray
‡ hearken to what *Dubartas* sings (for the hearing of such conjugal
25 faithfulness, will be Musick to all chaste ears) and therefore, I say,
hearken to what *Dubartas* sings of the *Mullet*:

> *But for chaste love the* Mullet *hath no peer,*
> *For, if the Fisher hath surprised her pheer,*
> *As mad with wo, to shoare she followeth,*
30 > *Prest to consort him both in life and death.*

On the contrary, what shall I say of the *House-Cock*, which treads
any Hen, and then (contrary to the *Swan*, the *Partridg*, and *Pigeon*)
takes no care to hatch, to feed, or to cherish his own Brood, but
is sensless though they perish.

† Rom. 2.14, 15.
‡ *Dubartas* 5. day.

And 'tis considerable, that the *Hen* (which because she also takes any *Cock*, expects it not) who is sure the Chickens be her own, hath by a moral impression her care, and affection to her own Broode, more then doubled, even to such a height, that our Saviour in expressing his love to *Jerusalem*, quotes her for an example of tender 5 affection, as his Father had done *Job* for a pattern of patience. †

And to parallel this *Cock*, there be divers fishes that cast their spawne on flags or stones, and then leave it uncovered and exposed to become a prey, and be devoured by Vermine or other fishes: but other fishes (as namely the *Barbel*) take such care for the preservation 10 of their seed, that (unlike to the *Cock* or the *Cuckoe*) they mutually labour (both the Spawner, and the Melter) to cover their spawne with sand, or watch it, or hide it in some secret place unfrequented by Vermine, or by any fish but themselves.

Sir, these examples may, to you and others, seem strange; but 15 they are testified, some by *Aristotle*, some by *Pliny*, some by *Gesner*, and by divers others of credit, and are believed and known by divers, both of wisdom and experience, to be a truth; and are (as I said at the beginning) fit for the contemplation of a most serious, and most pious man. 20

And that they be fit for the contemplation of the most prudent and pious, and peaceable men, seems to be testified by the practice of so many devout and contemplative men; as the Patriarks or Prophets of old, and of the Apostles of our Saviour in these later times, of which twelve he chose four that were Fishermen: 25 concerning which choice some have made these Observations.

First, That he never reproved these for their Imployment or Calling, as he did the Scribes and the Mony-Changers. And secondly, That he found the hearts of such men, men that by nature were fitted for contemplation and quietness; men of mild, and sweet, 30 and peaceable spirits, (as indeed most Anglers are) these men our blessed Saviour (who is observed to love to plant grace in good natures) though nothing be too hard for him, yet these men he chose to call from their irreprovable imployment, and gave them grace to be his Disciples and to follow him. 35

† Mat. 23, 37.

And it is observable, that it was our Saviours will that his four Fishermen Apostles should have a prioritie of nomination in the catalogue of his twelve Apostles, as namely first, S. *Peter*, *Andrew*,
† *James* and *John*, and then the rest in their order.

5   And it is yet more observable, that when our blessed Saviour went up into the Mount, at his Transfiguration, when he left the rest of his Disciples and chose onely three to bear him company, that these three were all Fisher-men.

And since I have your promise to hear me with patience, I will
10 take a liberty to look back upon an observation that hath been made by an ingenous and learned man, who observes that God hath been pleased to allow those whom he himselfe hath appointed, to write his holy will in holy Writ, yet to express his will in such Metaphors as their former affections or practise had inclined them
15 to; and he brings *Solomon* for an example, who before his conversion was remarkably amorous, and after by Gods appointment, writ that
‡ Love-Song betwixt God and his Church.

And if this hold in reason (as I see none to the contrary) then it may be probably concluded, that *Moses* (whom I told you before,
20 writ the book of *Job*) and the Prophet *Amos* were both Anglers, for you shal in all the old Testament, find fish-hooks but twice mentioned; namely, by meek *Moses*, the friend of God; and by the humble Prophet *Amos*.

Concerning which last, namely, the Prophet *Amos*, I shall make
25 but this Observation, That he that shall read the humble, lowly, plain stile of that Prophet, and compare it with the high, glorious, eloquent stile of the prophet *Isaiah* (though they are both equally true) may easily believe him to be a good natured, plaine Fisherman.

30 Which I do the rather believe, by comparing the affectionate, lowly, humble Epistles of S. *Peter*, S. *James* and S. *John*, whom we know were Fishers, with the glorious language and high Metaphors of S. *Paul*, whom we know was not.

Let me give you the example of two men more, that have lived
35 nearer to our own times: first of Doctor *Nowel* sometimes Dean of

† Mat. 10.
‡ The Canticles.

S. *Paul's*, (in which Church his Monument stands yet undefaced)
a man that in the Reformation of Queen *Elizabeth* (not that of *Henry
the VIII.*) was so noted for his meek spirit, deep Learning, Prudence
and Piety, that the then Parliament and Convocation, both chose,
injoyned, and trusted him to be the man to make a Catechism for 5
publick use, such a one as should stand as a rule for faith and
manners to their posteritie: And the good man (though he was very
learned, yet knowing that God leads us not to heaven by hard
questions) made that good, plain, unperplext Catechism, that is
printed with the old Service Book. I say, this good man was as dear 10
a lover, and constant practicer of Angling, as any Age can pro-
duce; and his custome was to spend, besides his fixt hours of prayer
(those hours which by command of the Church were enjoined the
old Clergy, and voluntarily dedicated to devotion by many
Primitive Christians:) besides those hours, this good man was 15
observed to spend, or if you will, to bestow a tenth part of his time
in Angling; and also (for I have conversed with those which have
conversed with him) to bestow a tenth part of his Revenue, and
all his fish, amongst the poor that inhabited near to those Rivers
in which it was caught, saying often, *That Charity gave life to Religion*: 20
and at his return would praise God he had spent that day free from
worldly trouble, both harmlesly and in a Recreation that became
a Church-man.

My next and last example shall be that undervaluer of money,
the late Provost of *Eaton Colledg*, Sir *Henry Wotton*, (a man with whom 25
I have often fish'd and convers'd) a man whose forraign imploy-
ments in the service of this Nation, and whose experience, learning,
wit and cheerfulness, made his company to be esteemed one of the
delights of mankind; this man, whose very approbation of Angling
were sufficient to convince any modest Censurer of it, this man was 30
also a most dear lover, and a frequent practicer of the Art of Angling,
of which he would say, "Twas an imployment for his idle time,
which was not idly spent'; for Angling was after tedious study 'A
rest to his mind, a cheerer of his spirits, a diversion of sadness, a
calmer of unquiet thoughts, a Moderator of passions, a procurer 35
of contentedness, and that it begot habits of peace and patience
in those that profest and practic'd it.'

Sir, This was the saying of that Learned man; and I do easily believe that peace, and patience, and a calm content did cohabit in the cheerful heart of Sir *Henry Wotton*, because I know, that when he was beyond seventy years of age he made this description of
5 a part of the present pleasure that possest him, as he sate quietly in a Summers evening on a bank a fishing; it is a description of the Spring, which because it glides as soft and sweetly from his pen, as that River does not by which it was then made, I shall repeat unto you.

10
  This day dame Nature seem'd in love:
  The lustie sap began to move;
  Fresh juice did stir th'imbracing Vines,
  And birds had drawn their Valentines.
  The jealous Trout, *that low did lye,*
15
  Rose at a well dissembled flie*;*
  There stood my friend with patient skill,
  Attending of his trembling quil.
  Already were the eaves possest
  With the swift Pilgrims dawbed nest:
20
  The Groves already did rejoice,
  In Philomels *triumphing voice:*
  The showrs were short, the weather mild,
  The morning fresh, the evening smil'd.
   Jone *takes her neat rubb'd pail, and now*
25
  She trips to milk the sand-red Cow;
  Where, for some sturdy foot-ball Swain,
  Jone *strokes a* Sillibub *or twaine.*
  The fields and gardens were beset
  With Tulips, Crocus, Violet,
30
  And now, though late, the modest Rose
  Did more then half a blush disclose.
  Thus all looks gay and full of chear
  To welcome the new liveried year.

These were the thoughts that then possest the undisturbed mind
† 35 of Sir *Henry Wotton*. Will you hear the wish of another Angler, and the commendation of his happy life, which he also sings in Verse?

† Jo. Da.

Let me live harmlesly, and near the brink
Of Trent or Avon have a dwelling place,
Where I may see my quil or cork down sink,
With eager bit of Pearch, or Bleak, or Dace;
And on the world and my Creator think,   5
Whilst some men strive, ill gotten goods t'imbrace;
    And others spend their time in base excess
    Of wine or worse, in war and wantonness.

Let them that list these pastimes still pursue,
And on such pleasing fancies feed their fill,   10
So I the fields and meadows green may view,
And daily by fresh Rivers walk at will,
Among the Daisies and the Violets blue,
Red Hyacinth, and yellow Daffadil,
    Purple Narcissus, like the morning rayes,   15
    Pale ganderglass and azure Culverkayes.

I count it higher pleasure to behold
The stately compass of the lofty Skie,
And in the the midst thereof (like burning Gold)
The flaming Chariot of the worlds great eye,   20
The watry clouds, that in the aire up rold,
With sundry kinds of painted colours flye;
    And fair Aurora lifting up her head,
    Still blushing, rise from old Tithonius bed.

The hils and mountains raised from the plains,   25
The plains extended level with the ground,
The grounds divided into sundry vains,
The vains inclos'd with rivers running round;
These rivers making way through natures chains
With headlong course into the sea profound;   30
    The raging sea, beneath the vallies low,
    Where lakes, and rils, and rivulets do flow.

The loftie woods, the Forrests wide and long
Adorn'd with leaves and branches fresh and green,
In whose cool bowres the birds with many a song   35
Do welcom with their Quire the Summers Queen:
The Meadows fair, where Flora's gifts among
Are intermixt, with verdant grass between.

The silver-scaled fish *that softly swim,*
Within the sweet brooks chrystal watry stream.

All these, and many more of his Creation,
That made the Heavens, the Angler *oft doth see,*
5 *Taking therein no little delectation,*
To think how strange, how wonderful they be;
Framing thereof an inward contemplation,
To set his heart from other fancies free;
And whilst he looks on these with joyful eye,
10 *His mind is rapt above the Starry Skie.*

Sir, I am glad my memory did not lose these last Verses, because they are somewhat more pleasant and more sutable to *May Day*, then my harsh Discourse, and I am glad your patience hath held out so long, as to hear them and me; for both together have brought 15 us within the sight of the *Thatcht House*; and I must be your Debtor (if you think it worth your attention) for the rest of my promised discourse, till some other opportunity and a like time of leisure.

Viat. Sir, You have Angled me on with much pleasure to the *thatcht House,* and I now find your words true, *That good company* 20 *makes the way seem short*; for, trust me, Sir, I thought we had wanted three miles of the *thatcht House*, till you shewed it me: but now we are at it, we'l turn into it, and refresh our selves with a cup of Ale and a little rest.

Pisc. Most gladly (Sir) and we'l drink a civil cup to all the 25 *Otter Hunters* that are to meet you to morrow.

Viat. That we wil, Sir, and to all the lovers of Angling too, of which number, I am now one my self, for by the help of your good discourse and company, I have put on new thoughts both of the Art of Angling, and of all that profess it: and if you will but meet 30 me too morrow at the time and place appointed, and bestow one day with me and my friends in hunting the *Otter*, I will the next two dayes wait upon you, and we two will for that time do nothing but angle, and talk of fish and fishing.

Pisc. 'Tis a match, Sir, I'l not fail you, God willing, to be at 35 *Amwel Hil* to morrow morning before Sun-rising.

CHAP. II.

Viat. My friend *Piscator*, you have kept time with my thoughts, for the Sun is just rising, and I my self just now come to this place, and the dogs have just now put down an *Otter*; look down at the bottom of the hil, there in that Meadow, chequered with water 5 Lillies and Lady-smocks, there you may see what work they make: look, you see all busie, men and dogs, dogs and men, all busie.

Pisc. Sir, I am right glad to meet you, and glad to have so fair an entrance into this dayes sport, and glad to see so many dogs, and more men all in pursuit of the *Otter*; lets complement no longer, 10 but joine unto them; come honest *Viator*, lets be gone, lets make haste, I long to be doing; no reasonable hedge or ditch shall hold me.

Viat. Gentleman Huntsman, where found you this *Otter*?

Hunt. Marry (Sir) we found her a mile off this place a fishing; 15 she has this morning eaten the greatest part of this *Trout*, she has only left thus much of it as you see, and was fishing for more; when we came we found her just at it; but we were here very early, we were here an hour before Sun-rise, and have given her no rest since we came: sure she'l hardly escape all these dogs and men. I am 20 to have the skin if we kill him.

Viat. Why, Sir, whats the skin worth?

Hunt. 'Tis worth ten shillings to make gloves; the gloves of an *Otter* are the best fortification for your hands against wet weather that can be thought of. 25

Pisc. I pray, honest Huntsman, let me ask you a pleasant question, Do you hunt a Beast or a fish?

Hunt. Sir, It is not in my power to resolve you; for the question has been debated among many Clerks, and they seem to differ about it; but most agree, that his tail is fish: and if his body be 30 fish too, then I may say, that fish will walk upon land (for an *Otter* does so) sometimes five or six, or ten miles in a night. But (Sir) I can tell you certainly, that he devours much fish, and kils and

39

spoils much more: And I can tell you, that he can smel a fish in the water one hundred yards from him (*Gesner* sayes, much farther) and that his stones are good against the Falling-sickness: and that there is an herb *Benione*, which being hung in a linen cloth
5 near a Fish Pond, or any haunt that he uses, makes him to avoid the place, which proves he can smell both by water and land. And thus much for my knowledge of the *Otter*, which you may now see above water at vent, and the dogs close with him; I now see he will not last long, follow therefore my Masters, follow, for *Sweetlips*
10 was like to have him at this vent.

Viat. Oh me, all the Horse are got over the river, what shall we do now?

Hunt. Marry, stay a little and follow, both they and the dogs will be suddenly on this side again, I warrant you, and the *Otter*
15 too it may be: now have at him with *Kilbuck*, for he vents again.

Viat. Marry so he is, for look he vents in that corner. Now, now *Ringwood* has him. Come bring him to me. Look, 'tis a Bitch *Otter* upon my word, and she has lately whelped, lets go to the place where she was *put down*, and not far from it, you will find all her
20 young ones, I dare warrant you: and kill them all too.

Hunt. Come Gentlemen, come all, lets go to the place where we *put downe* the *Otter*; look you, hereabout it was that shee kennell'd; look you, here it was indeed, for here's her young ones, no less then five: come lets kill them all.

25 *Pisc.* No, I pray Sir; save me one, and I'll try if I can make her
† tame, as I know an ingenuous Gentleman in *Leicester-shire* has done; who hath not only made her tame, but to catch fish, and doe many things of much pleasure.

Hunt. Take one with all my heart; but let us kill the rest. And
30 now lets go to an honest Alehouse and sing *Old Rose*, and rejoice all of us together.

Viat. Come my friend, let me invite you along with us; I'll bear your charges this night, and you shall beare mine to morrow; for my intention is to accompany you a day or two in fishing.

† *Mr Nich. Seagrave.*

Pisc. Sir, you request is granted, and I shall be right glad, both to exchange such a courtesie, and also to enjoy your company.

Viat. Well, now lets go to your sport of Angling.

Pisc. Let's be going with all my heart, God keep you all, Gentlemen, and send you meet this day with another bitch *Otter*, and kill her merrily, and all her young ones too.

Viat. Now *Piscator*, where wil you begin to fish?

Pisc. We are not yet come to a likely place, I must walk a mile further yet before I begin.

Viat. Well then, I pray, as we walk, tell me freely how do you like my Hoste, and the company? is not mine Hoste a witty man?

Pisc. Sir, To speak truly, he is not to me; for most of his conceits were either Scripture-jests, or lascivious jests; for which I count no man witty: for the Divel will help a man that way inclin'd, to the first, and his own corrupt nature (which he always carries with him) to the latter. But a companion that feasts the company with *wit* and *mirth*, and leaves out the *sin* (which is usually mixt with them) he is the man: and indeed, such a man should have his charges born: and to such company I hope to bring you this night; for at *Trout-Hal*, not far from this place, where I purpose to lodg to night, there is usually an Angler that proves good company.

But for such discourse as we heard last night, it infects others; the very boyes will learn to talk and swear as they heard mine Host, and another of the company that shall be nameless; well, you know what example is able to do, and I know what the Poet sayes in the like case:

> —— *Many a one*
> *Owes to his Country his Religion:*
> *And in another would as strongly grow,*
> *Had but his Nurse or Mother taught him so.*

This is reason put into Verse, and worthy the consideration of a wise man. But of this no more, for though I love civility, yet I hate severe censures: I'll to my own Art, and I doubt not but at yonder tree I shall catch a *Chub*, and then we'll turn to an honest cleanly

Ale house that I know right well, rest our selves, and dress it for our dinner.

Viat. Oh, Sir, a *Chub* is the worst fish that swims, I hoped for a *Trout* for my dinner.

5 *Pisc.* Trust me, Sir, there is not a likely place for a *Trout* hereabout, and we staid so long to take our leave of your Huntsmen this morning, that the Sun is got so high, and shines so clear, that I will not undertake the catching of a *Trout* till evening; and though a *Chub* be by you and many others reckoned the worst of all fish,
10 yet you shall see I'll make it good fish by dressing it.

Viat. Why, how will you dress him?

Pisc. I'l tell you when I have caught him: look you here, Sir, do you see? (but you must stand very close) there lye upon the top of the water twenty *Chubs*: I'll catch only one, and that shall be the
15 biggest of them all: and that I will do so, I'll hold you twenty to one.

Viat. I marry, Sir, now you talk like an Artist, and I'll say, you are one, when I shall see you perform what you say you can do; but I yet doubt it.

Pisc. And that you shall see me do presently; look, the biggest
20 of these *Chubs* has had some bruise upon his tail, and that looks like a white spot; that very *Chub* I mean to catch; sit you but down in the shade, and stay but a little while, and I'l warrant you I'l bring him to you.

Viat. I'l sit down and hope well, because you seem to be so
25 confident.

Pisc. Look you Sir, there he is, that very *Chub* that I shewed you, with the white spot on his tail; and I'l be as certain to make him a good dish of meat, as I was to catch him. I'l now lead you to an honest Alehouse, where we shall find a cleanly room, Lavender
30 in the windowes, and twenty Ballads stuck about the wall; there my Hostis (which I may tel you, is both cleanly and conveniently handsome) has drest many a one for me, and shall now dress it after my fashion, and I warrant it good meat.

Viat. Come Sir, with all my heart, for I begin to be hungry, and
35 long to be at it, and indeed to rest my self too; for though I have walk'd but four miles this morning, yet I begin to be weary; yester dayes hunting hangs stil upon me.

Pisc. Wel Sir, and you shal quickly be at rest, for yonder is the house I mean to bring you to.

Come Hostis, how do you? wil you first give us a cup of your best Ale, and then dress this *Chub*, as you drest my last, when I and my friend were here about eight or ten daies ago? but you 5 must do me one courtesie, it must be done instantly.

Host. I will do it, Mr *Piscator*, and with all the speed I can.

Pisc. Now Sir, has not my Hostis made haste? and does not the fish look lovely?

Viat. Both, upon my word Sir, and therefore lets say Grace and 10 fall to eating of it.

Pisc. Well Sir, how do you like it?

Viat. Trust me, 'tis as good meat as ever I tasted: now let me thank you for it, drink to you, and beg a courtesie of you; but it must not be deny'd me. 15

Pisc. What is it, I pray Sir? you are so modest, that me thinks I may promise to grant it before it is asked.

Viat. Why Sir, it is that from henceforth you will allow me to call you Master, and that really I may be your Scholer, for you are such a companion, and have so quickly caught, and so ex- 20 cellently cook'd this fish, as makes me ambitious to be your scholer.

Pisc. Give me your hand: from this time forward I wil be your Master, and teach you as much of this Art as I am able; and will, as you desire me, tel you somewhat of the nature of some of the fish which we are to Angle for; and I am sure I shal tel you more 25 then every Angler yet knows.

And first I will tel you how you shall catch such a *Chub* as this way; and then how to cook him as this was: I could not have begun to teach you to catch any fish more easily then this fish is caught; but then it must be this particular way, and this you must do: 30

Go to the same hole, where in most hot days you will finde floting neer the top of the water, at least a dozen or twenty *Chubs*; get a *Grashopper* or two as you goe, and get secretly behinde the tree, put it then upon your hook, and let your hook hang a quarter of a yard short of the top of the water, and 'tis very likely that the shadow 35 of your rod, which you must rest on the tree, will cause the *Chubs* to sink down to the bottom with fear; for they be a very fearful

fish, and the shadow of a bird flying over them will make them do so; but they will presently rise up to the top again, and there lie soaring till some shadow affrights them again: when they lie upon the top of the water, look out the best *Chub*, which you setting your
5 self in a fit place, may very easily doe, and move your Rod as softly as a Snail moves, to that *Chub* you intend to catch; let your bait fall gently upon the water three or four inches before him, and he will infallibly take the bait, and you will be as sure to catch him; for hee is one of the leather-mouth'd fishes, of which a hook does
10 scarce ever lose his hold: and therefore give him play enough before you offer to take him out of the water. Go your way presently, take my rod, and doe as I bid you, and I will sit down and mend my tackling till you return back.

Viat. Truly, my loving Master, you have offered mee as fair as
15 I could wish: Ile goe and observe your directions.

Look you, Master, what I have done; that which joyes my heart; caught just such another *Chub* as yours was.

Pisc. Marry, and I am glad of it: I am like to have a towardly Scholer of you. I now see, that with advice and practice you wil
20 make an *Angler* in a short time.

Viat. But Master, What if I could not have found a *Grashopper*?

Pisc. Then I may tel you, that a *black Snail*, with his belly slit, to shew his white; or a piece of soft *cheese* wil usually do as wel; nay, sometimes a *worm*, or any kind of *fly*; as the *Ant-fly*, the *Flesh-fly*,
25 or *Wall-fly*, or the *Dor* or *Beetle*, (which you may find under a Cowturd) or a *Bob*, which you wil find in the same place, and in time wil be a *Beetle*; it is a short white worm, like to, and bigger then a Gentle; or a *Cod-worm*, or *Case-worm*: any of these wil do very wel to fish in such a manner. And after this manner you may catch
30 a *Trout*: in a hot evening, when as you walk by a Brook, and shal see or hear him leap at Flies, then if you get a *Grashopper*, put it on your hook, with your line about two yards long, standing behind a bush or tree where his hole is, and make your bait stir up and down on the top of the water; you may, if you stand close, be sure
35 of a bit, but not sure to catch him, for he is not a leather mouthed fish: and after this manner you may fish for him with almost any kind of live Flie, but especially with a *Grashopper*.

Viat. But before you go further, I pray good Master, what mean you by a leather mouthed fish?

Pisc. By a leather mouthed fish, I mean such as have their teeth in their throat, as the *Chub* or *Cheven*, and so the *Barbel*, the *Gudgion* and *Carp*, and divers others have; and the hook being stuck into the leather or skin of such fish, does very seldome or never lose its hold: But on the contrary, a *Pike*, a *Pearch*, or *Trout*, and so some other fish which have not their teeth in their throats, but in their mouthes, which you shal observe to be very full of bones, and the skin very thin, and little of it: I say, of these fish the hook never takes so sure hold, but you often lose the fish unless he have gorg'd it.

Viat. I thank you good Master for this observation; but now what shal be done with my *Chub* or *Cheven* that I have caught?

Pisc. Marry Sir, it shall be given away to some poor body, for Ile warrant you Ile give you a *Trout* for your supper; and it is a good beginning of your Art to offer your first fruits to the poor, who will both thank God and you for it.

And now lets walk towards the water again, and as I go Ile tel you when you catch your next *Chub*, how to dresse it as this was.

Viat. Come (good Master) I long to be going and learn your direction.

Pisc. You must dress it, or see it drest thus: When you have scaled him, wash him very cleane, cut off his tail and fins; and wash him not after you gut him, but chine or cut him through the middle as a salt fish is cut, then give him four or five scotches with your knife, broil him upon wood-cole or char-cole; but as he is broiling, baste him often with butter that shal be choicely good; and put good store of salt into your butter, or salt him gently as you broil or baste him; and bruise or cut very smal into your butter, a little Time, or some other sweet herb that is in the Garden where you eat him: thus used, it takes away the watrish taste which the *Chub* or *Chevin* has, and makes him a choice dish of meat, as you your self know; for thus was that dress'd, which you did eat of to your dinner.

Or you may (for variety) dress a *Chub* another way, and you wil find him very good, and his tongue and head almost as good as a Carps; but then you must be sure that no grasse or weeds be left in his mouth or throat.

Thus you must dress him: Slit him through the middle, then cut him into four pieces; then put him into a pewter dish, and cover him with another, put into him as much White Wine as wil cover him, or Spring water and Vinegar, and store of Salt, with some branches of Time, and other sweet herbs; let him then be boiled gently over a Chafing-dish with wood coles, and when he is almost boiled enough, put half of the liquor from him, not the top of it; put then into him a convenient quantity of the best butter you can get, with a little Nutmeg grated into it, and sippets of white bread: thus ordered, you wil find the *Chevin* and the sauce too, a choice dish of meat: And I have been the more careful to give you a perfect direction how to dress him, because he is a fish undervalued by many, and I would gladly restore him to some of his credit which he has lost by ill Cookery.

Viat. But Master, have you no other way to catch a *Cheven*, or *Chub?*

Pisc. Yes that I have, but I must take time to tel it you hereafter; or indeed, you must learn it by observation and practice, though this way that I have taught you was the easiest to catch a *Chub*, at this time, and at this place. And now we are come again to the River; I will (as the Souldier sayes) prepare for skirmish; that is, draw out my Tackling, and try to catch a *Trout* for supper.

Viat. Trust me Master, I see now it is a harder matter to catch a *Trout* then a *Chub*; for I have put on patience, and followed you this two hours, and not seen a fish stir, neither at your Minnow nor your Worm.

Pisc. Wel Scholer, you must indure worse luck sometime, or you will never make a good Angler. But what say you now? there is a *Trout* now, and a good one too, if I can but hold him; and two or three turns more will tire him: Now you see he lies still, and the sleight is to land him: Reach me that Landing net: So (Sir) now he is mine own, what say you? is not this worth all my labour?

Viat. On my word Master, this is a gallant *Trout*; what shall we do with him?

Pisc. Marry ee'n eat him to supper: We'l go to my Hostis, from whence we came; she told me, as I was going out of door, that my brother *Peter*, a good Angler, and a cheerful companion, had sent word he would lodg there to night, and bring a friend with him. My Hostis has two beds, and I know you and I may have the best: we'l rejoice with my brother *Peter* and his friend, tel tales, 5 or sing Ballads, or make a Catch, or find some harmless sport to content us.

Viat. A match, good Master, lets go to that house, for the linnen looks white, and smels of Lavender, and I long to lye in a pair of sheets that smels so: lets be going, good Master, for I am hungry 10 again with fishing.

Pisc. Nay, stay a little good Scholer, I caught my last *Trout* with a worm, now I wil put on a Minow and try a quarter of an hour about yonder trees for another, and so walk towards our lodging. Look you Scholer, thereabout we shall have a bit presently, or not 15 at all: Have with you (Sir!) on my word I have him. Oh it is a great logger-headed *Chub*: Come, hang him upon that Willow twig, and let's be going. But turn out of the way a little, good Scholer, towards yonder high hedg: We'l sit whilst this showr falls so gently upon the teeming earth, and gives a sweeter smel to the lovely 20 flowers that adorn the verdant Meadows.

Look, under that broad *Beech tree* I sate down when I was last this way a fishing, and the birds in the adjoining Grove seemed to have a friendly contention with an Echo, whose dead voice seemed to live in a hollow cave, near to the brow of that Primrose 25 hil; there I sate viewing the Silver streams glide silently towards their center, the tempestuous Sea, yet sometimes opposed by rugged roots, and pibble stones, which broke their waves, and turned them into fome: and sometimes viewing the harmless Lambs, some leaping securely in the cool shade, whilst others 30 sported themselvs in the cheerful Sun; and others were craving comfort from the swolne Udders of their bleating Dams. As I thus sate, these and other sights had so fully possest my soul, that I thought as the Poet has happily exprest it:

I was for that time lifted above earth; 35
And possest joyes not promis'd in my birth.

As I left this place, and entered into the next field, a second pleasure entertained me, 'twas a handsome Milk-maid, that had cast away all care, and sung like a *Nightingale*; her voice was good, and the Ditty fitted for it; 'twas that smooth Song which was made
5 by *Kit Marlow*, now at least fifty years ago; and the Milkmaids mother sung an answer to it, which was made by Sir *Walter Raleigh* in his younger dayes.

They were old fashioned Poetry, but choicely good, I think much better then that now in fashion in this Critical age. Look yonder,
10 on my word, yonder they be both a milking again: I wil give her the *Chub*, and perswade them to sing those two songs to us.

Pisc. God speed, good woman, I have been a fishing, and am going to *Bleak Hall* to my bed, and having caught more fish then wil sup my self and friend, wil bestow this upon you and your
15 daughter, for I use to sel none.

Milk. Marry God requite you Sir, and we'l eat it cheerfully: wil you drink a draught of red Cows milk?

Pisc. No, I thank you: but I pray do us a courtesie that shal stand you and your daughter in nothing, and we wil think our selves stil
20 something in your debt; it is but to sing us a Song, that that was sung by you and your daughter, when I last past over this Meadow, about eight or nine dayes since.

Milk. What Song was it, I pray? was it, *Come Shepherds deck your heads*: or, *As at noon* Dulcina *rested*: or *Philida flouts me*?
25 *Pisc.* No, it is none of those: it is a Song that your daughter sung the first part, and you sung the answer to it.

Milk. O I know it now, I learn'd the first part in my golden age, when I was about the age of my daughter; and the later part, which indeed fits me best, but two or three years ago; you shal,
30 God willing, hear them both. Come *Maudlin*, sing the first part to the Gentlemen with a merrie heart, and Ile sing the second.

The Milk maids Song.

Come live with me, and be my Love,
And we wil all the pleasures prove
35 *That vallies, Groves, or hils, or fields,*
Or woods and steepie mountains yeelds.

48

Where we will sit upon the Rocks,
And see the Shepherds feed our flocks,
By shallow River, *to whose falls*
Mellodious birds sing madrigals.

And I wil make thee beds of Roses,   5
And then a thousand fragrant posies,
A cap of flowers and a Kirtle,
Imbroidered all with leaves of Mirtle.

A Gown made of the finest wool
Which from our pretty Lambs we pull,   10
Slippers lin'd choicely for the cold,
With buckles of the purest gold.

A belt of straw and ivie buds,
With Coral clasps, and Amber studs:
And if these pleasures may thee move,   15
Come live with me, and be my Love.

The Shepherds Swains shal dance and sing
For thy delight each May morning:
If these delights thy mind may move,
Then live with me, and be my Love.   20

Viat. Trust me Master, it is a choice Song, and sweetly sung by honest *Maudlin*: Ile bestow Sir *Thomas Overbury's* Milk maids wish upon her, *That she may dye in the Spring, and have good store of flowers stuck round about her winding sheet.*

The Milk maids mothers answer.   25

If all the world and love were young,
And truth in every Shepherds tongue?
These pretty pleasures might me move,
To live with thee, and be thy love.

But time drives flocks from field to fold: 30
When rivers rage and rocks grow cold,
And Philomel *becometh dumb,*
The Rest complains of cares to come.

The Flowers do fade, and wanton fields
To wayward Winter reckoning yeilds.
A honey tongue, a heart of gall,
Is fancies spring, but sorrows fall.

5   *Thy gowns, thy shooes, thy beds of Roses,*
Thy Cap, thy Kirtle, and thy Posies,
Soon break, soon wither, soon forgotten,
In folly ripe, in reason rotten.

Thy belt of straw and Ivie buds,
10   *Thy Coral clasps and Amber studs,*
All these in me no means can move
To come to thee, and be thy Love.

But could youth last, and love stil breed,
Had joyes no date, nor age no need;
15   *Then those delights my mind might move*
To live with thee, and be thy love.

Pisc. Wel sung, good woman, I thank you, I'l give you another dish of fish one of these dayes, and then beg another Song of you. Come Scholer, let *Maudlin* alone, do not you offer to spoil her voice. 20 Look, yonder comes my Hostis to cal us to supper. How now? is my brother *Peter* come?

Host. Yes, and a friend with him, they are both glad to hear you are in these parts, and long to see you, and are hungry, and long to be at supper.

Pisc. Wel met brother *Peter*, I heard you and a friend would lodg here to night, and that has made me and my friend cast to lodge here too; my friend is one that would faine be a brother of the *Angle*: he has been an *Angler* but this day, and I have taught him how 5 to catch a *Chub* by *daping* with a *Grashopper*, and he has caught a lusty one of nineteen inches long. But I pray you brother, who is it that is your companion?

Pet. Brother *Piscator*, my friend is an honest Country man, and his name is *Coridon*, a most downright witty merry companion that 10 met me here purposely to eat a *Trout* and be pleasant, and I have not yet wet my line since I came from home: But I wil fit him to morrow with a *Trout* for his breakfast, if the weather be any thing like.

Pisc. Nay brother, you shall not delay him so long, for look you 15 here is a *Trout* will fill six reasonable bellies. Come Hostis, dress it presently, and get us what other meat the house will afford, and give us some good Ale, and lets be merrie.

Pet. On my word, this *Trout* is in perfect season. Come, I thank 20 you, and here's a hearty draught to you, and to all the brothers of the Angle, wheresoever they be, and to my young brothers good fortune to morrow; I wil furnish him with a rod, if you wil furnish him with the rest of the tackling, we wil set him up and make him a fisher.

And I wil tel him one thing for his encouragement, that his fortune hath made him happy to be a Scholer to such a Master; a Master that knowes as much both of the nature and breeding of fish, as any man; and can also tell him as well how to catch and cook them, from the *Minow* to the *Sammon*, as any that I ever met withall.

Pisc. Trust me, brother *Peter*, I find my Scholer to be so sutable to my own humour, which is to be free and pleasant, and civilly merry, that my resolution is to hide nothing from him. Believe me, Scholer, this is my resolution: and so here's to you a hearty draught, and to all that love us, and the honest Art of Angling.

Viat. Trust me, good Master, you shall not sow your seed in barren ground, for I hope to return you an increase answerable to your hopes; but however, you shal find me obedient, and thankful, and serviceable to my best abilitie.

Pisc. 'Tis enough, honest Scholer, come lets to supper. Come my friend *Coridon*, this *Trout* looks lovely, it was twenty two inches when it was taken, and the belly of it look'd some part of it as yellow as a Marygold, and part of it as white as a Lily, and yet me thinks it looks better in this good sawce.

Coridon. Indeed, honest friend, it looks well, and tastes well, I thank you for it, and so does my friend *Peter*, or else he is to blame.

Pet. Yes, and so I do, we all thank you, and when we have supt, I wil get my friend *Coridon* to sing you a Song, for requital.

Cor. I wil sing a Song if any body wil sing another; else, to be plain with you, I wil sing none: I am none of those that sing for meat, but for company; I say, 'Tis merry in Hall when men sing all.

Pisc. I'l promise you I'l sing a Song that was lately made at my request by Mr *William Basse*, one that has made the choice Songs of the *Hunter in his carrere*, and of *Tom of Bedlam*, and many others of note; and this that I wil sing is in praise of Angling.

Cor. And then mine shall be the praise of a Country mans life: What will the rest sing of?

Pet. I wil promise you I wil sing another Song in praise of Angling, to morrow night, for we wil not part till then, but fish to morrow, and sup together, and the next day every man leave fishing, and fall to his business.

Viat. Tis a match, and I wil provide you a Song or a Ketch against then too, that shal give some addition of mirth to the company; for we wil be merrie.

Pisc. Tis a match my masters; lets ev'n say Grace, and turn to the fire, drink the other cup to wet our whistles, and so sing away all sad thoughts.

Come on my masters, who begins? I think it is best to draw cuts and avoid contention.

Pet. It is a match. Look, the shortest Cut fals to *Coridon.*

Cor. Well then, I wil begin; for I hate contention.

CORIDONS SONG.

Oh the sweet contentment
The country man doth find!
    high trolollie loliloe
    high trolollie lee,
That quiet contemplation
possesseth all my mind:
    Then care away,
    and wend along with me.

For Courts are full of flattery,
As hath too oft been tri'd;
    high trolollie lollie loe
    high trolollie lee,
The City full of wantonness,
and both are full of pride:
    Then care away,
    and wend along with me.

But oh the honest country man
Speaks truly from his heart,
    high trolollie lollie loe
    high trolollie lee,
His pride is in his Tillage,
his Horses and his Cart:
    Then care away,
    and wend along with me.

Our clothing is good sheep skins
Gray russet for our wives,
  high trolollie lollie loe
  high trolollie lee.
5 *'Tis warmth and not gay clothing*
that doth prolong our lives:
  Then care away,
  and wend along with me.

The ploughman, though he labor hard,
10 *Yet on the* Holy-day,
  high trolollie lollie loe
  high trolollie lee,
No Empéror *so merrily*
does pass his time away:
15 Then care away,
  and wend along with me.

To recompence our Tillage,
The Heavens *afford us showrs;*
  high trolollie lollie loe
20 *high trolollie lee,*
And for our sweet refreshments
the earth affords us bowers:
  Then care away, &c.

The Cuckoe *and the* Nightingale
25 *full merrily do sing,*
  high trolollie lollie loe
  high trolollie lee,
And with their pleasant roundelayes,
bid welcome to the Spring:
30 Then care away,
  and wend along with me.

This is not half the happiness
the Country man injoyes;
  high trolollie lollie loe
35 *high trolollie lee,*
Though others think they have as much
yet he that sayes so lies:
  Then come away, turn
  Country man with me.

Pisc. Well sung *Coridon*, this Song was sung with mettle, and it was choicely fitted to the occasion; I shall love you for it as long as I know you: I would you were a brother of the Angle, for a companion that is cheerful and free from swearing and scurrilous discourse, is worth gold. I love such mirth as does not make friends 5 ashamed to look upon one another next morning; nor men (that cannot wel bear it) to repent the money they spend when they be warmed with drink: and take this for a rule, you may pick out such times and such companies, that you may make your selves merrier for a little then a great deal of money; for *'Tis the company* 10 *and not the charge that makes the feast*: and such a companion you prove, I thank you for it.

But I will not complement you out of the debt that I owe you, and therefore I will begin my Song, and wish it may be as well liked. 15

THE ANGLERS SONG.

As inward love breeds outward talk,
The Hound *some praise, and some the* Hawk,
Some better pleas'd with private sport,
Use Tenis, *some a* Mistris *court:* 20
* But these delights I neither wish,*
* Nor envy, while I freely fish.*

Who hunts, *doth oft in danger ride;*
Who hauks, *lures oft both far and wide;*
Who uses games, *may often prove* 25
A loser; but who fals in love,
* Is fettered in fond* Cupids *snare:*
* My Angle breeds me no such care.*

Of Recreation there is none
So free as fishing is alone; 30
All other pastimes do no less
Then mind and body both possess;
* My hand alone my work can do,*
* So I can fish and study too.*

I care not, I, to fish in seas, 35
Fresh rivers best my mind do please,

Whose sweet calm course I contemplate,
And seek in life to imitate;
* In civil bounds I fain would keep,*
* And for my past offences weep.*

5   *And when the timerous* Trout *I wait*
To take, and he devours my bait,
How poor a thing sometimes I find
Will captivate a greedy mind:
* And when none bite, I praise the wise,*
10 * Whom vain alurements ne're surprise.*

But yet though while I fish, I fast,
I make good fortune my repast,
And thereunto my friend invite,
In whom I more then that delight:
15 * Who is more welcome to my dish,*
* Then to my Angle was my fish.*

As well content no prize to take
As use of taken prize to make;
For so our Lord was pleased when
20 *He Fishers made Fishers of men;*
* Where (which is in no other game)*
* A man may fish and praise his name.*

The first men that our Saviour dear
Did chuse to wait upon him here,
25 *Blest Fishers were; and fish the last*
Food was, that he on earth did taste:
* I therefore strive to follow those,*
* Whom he to follow him hath chose.*

                                    W.B.

Cor. Well sung brother, you have paid your debt in good coyn,
30 we Anglers are all beholding to the good man that made this Song.
Come Hostis, give us more Ale and lets drink to him.

And now lets everie one go to bed that we may rise early; but
first lets pay our Reckoning, for I wil have nothing to hinder me
in the morning, for I will prevent the Sun-rising.

35   *Pet.* A match: Come *Coridon*, you are to be my Bed-fellow: I know

brother you and your Scholer wil lie together; but where shal we meet to morrow night? for my friend *Coridon* and I will go up the water towards *Ware*.

Pisc. And my Scholer and I will go down towards *Waltam*.

Cor. Then lets meet here, for here are fresh sheets that smel of 5 Lavender, and I am sure, we cannot expect better meat and better usage.

Pet. 'Tis a match. Good night to every body.

Pisc. And so say I.

Viat. And so say I.   10

Pisc. Good morrow good Hostis, I see my brother *Peter* is in bed still; Come, give my Scholer and me a cup of Ale, and be sure you get us a good dish of meat against supper, for we shall come hither as hungry as *Hawks*. Come Scholer, lets be going.

Viat. Good Master, as we walk towards the water, wil you be 15 pleased to make the way seeme shorter by telling me first the nature of the *Trout*, and then how to catch him.

Pisc. My honest Scholer, I wil do it freely: The *Trout* (for which I love to angle above any fish) may be justly said (as the ancient Poets say of Wine, and we English say of Venison) to be a generous 20 fish, because he has his seasons, a fish that comes in, and goes out with the *Stag* or *Buck*: and you are to observe, that as there be some *barren Does*, that are good in Summer; so there be some *barren Trouts*, that are good in Winter; but there are not many that are so, for usually they be in their perfection in the month of *May*, and decline 25 with the *Buck*: Now you are to take notice, that in several Countries, as in *Germany* and in other parts compar'd to ours, they differ much in their bigness, shape and other wayes, and so do *Trouts*; 'tis wel known that in the Lake *Lemon*, the Lake of *Geneva*, there are *Trouts* taken, of three Cubits long, as is affirmed by *Gesner*, a Writer of 30 good credit: and *Mercator* sayes, the *Trouts* that are taken in the Lake of *Geneva*, are a great part of the Merchandize of that famous City. And you are further to know, that there be certaine waters that breed *Trouts* remarkable, both for their number and smalness. I know a little Brook in *Kent* that breeds them to a number 35 incredible, and you make take them twentie or fortie in an hour,

but none greater then about the size of a *Gudgion*. There are also in divers Rivers, especially that relate to, or be near to the Sea, (as *Winchester*, or the Thames about *Windsor*) a little *Trout* called a *Samlet* or *Skegger Trout* (in both which places I have caught twentie
5 or fortie at a standing) that will bite as fast and as freely as *Minnows*; these be by some taken to be young *Salmons*, but in those waters they never grow to bee bigger then a *Herring*.

There is also in *Kent*, neer to *Canterbury*, a *Trout* (called there a *Fordig Trout*) a *Trout* (that bears the name of the Town where
10 'tis usually caught) that is accounted rare meat, many of them near the bigness of a Salmon, but knowne by their different colour, and in their best season cut very white; and none have been known to be caught with an Angle, unless it were one that was caught by honest Sir *George Hastings*, an excellent Angler (and now with
15 God) and he has told me, he thought that *Trout* bit not for hunger, but wantonness; and 'tis the rather to be believed, because both he then, and many others before him have been curious to search into their bellies what the food was by which they lived; and have found out nothing by which they might satisfie their curiositie.

20 Concerning which you are to take notice, that it is reported, there is a fish that hath not any mouth, but lives by taking breath by the poriness of her gils, and feeds and is nourish'd by no man knows what; and this may be believed of the *Fordig Trout*, which (as it is said of the *Stork*, that he knowes his season, so he) knows his times
25 (I think almost his day) of coming into that River out of the Sea, where he lives (and it is like feeds) nine months of the year, and about three in the River of *Fordig*.

And now for some confirmation of this; you are to know, that this *Trout* is thought to eat nothing in the fresh water; and it may
30 be the better believed, because it is well known, that *Swallowes*, which are not seen to flye in *England* for six months in the year, but about *Michaelmas* leave us for a hotter climate; yet some of them, that have been left behind their fellows, have been found (many thousand at a time) in hollow trees, where they have been observed to
† 35 live and sleep out the whole winter without meat; and so *Albertus*

† View Sir *Fra. Bacon* exper. 899.
‡ See *Topsel* of *Frogs*.

observes that there is one kind of *Frog* that hath her mouth naturally shut up about the end of *August*, and that she lives so all the Winter, and though it be strange to some, yet it is known to too many amongst us to bee doubted.

And so much for these *Fordidg Trouts*, which never afford an 5 *Angler* sport, but either live their time of being in the fresh water by their meat formerly gotten in the Sea, (not unlike the *Swallow* or *Frog*) or by the vertue of the fresh water only, as the *Camelion* is said to live by the air.

There is also in *Northumberland*, a *Trout*, called a *Bull Trout*, of 10 a much greater length and bignesse then any in these Southern parts; and there is in many Rivers that relate to the Sea, *Salmon Trouts* as much different one from another, both in shape and in their spots, as we see Sheep differ one from another in their shape and bigness, and in the fineness of their wool: and certainly as some 15 Pastures do breed larger Sheep, so do some Rivers, by reason of the ground over which they run, breed larger *Trouts*.

Now the next thing I will commend to your consideration is, That the *Trout* is of a more sudden growth then other fish: concerning which you are also to take notice, that he lives not so long 20 as the *Pearch* and divers other fishes do, as Sir *Francis Bacon* hath observed in his History of life and death.

And next, you are to take notice, that after hee is come to his full growth, he declines in his bodie, but keeps his bigness or thrives in his head till his death. And you are to know that he wil about 25 (especially before) the time of his Spawning, get almost miraculously through *Weires* and *Floud-Gates* against the stream, even through such high and swift places as is almost incredible. Next, that the *Trout* usually Spawns about *October* or *November*, but in some Rivers a little sooner or later; which is the more observable, 30 because most other fish Spawne in the Spring or Summer, when the Sun hath warmed both the earth and water, and made it fit for generation.

And next, you are to note, that till the Sun gets to such a height as to warm the earth and the water, the *Trout* is sick, and lean, 35 and lowsie, and unwholsome: for you shall in winter find him to have a big head, and then to be lank, and thin, and lean; at which

time many of them have sticking on them Sugs, or *Trout* lice, which is a kind of worm, in shape like a Clove or a Pin, with a big head, and sticks close to him and sucks his moisture; those I think the *Trout* breeds himselfe, and never thrives til he free himself from
5 them, which is till warm weather comes, and then as he growes stronger, he gets from the dead, still water, into the sharp streames and the gravel and there rubs off these worms or lice: and then as he grows stronger, so he gets him into swifter and swifter streams, and there lies at the watch for any flie or Minow that comes neer
10 to him; and he especially loves the *May* flie, which is bred of the *Cod-worm* or *Caddis*; and these make the Trout bold and lustie, and he is usually fatter, and better meat at the end of that month, then at any time of the year.

Now you are to know, that it is observed, that usually the best
15 *Trouts* are either red or yellow, though some be white and yet good; but that is not usual; and it is a note observable that the female *Trout* hath usually a less head and a deeper body then the male *Trout*; and a little head to any fish, either *Trout*, *Salmon*, or other fish, is a sign that that fish is in season.

20 But yet you are to note, that as you see some Willows or Palm trees bud and blossome sooner then others do, so some *Trouts* be in some Rivers sooner in season; and as the Holly or Oak are longer before they cast their Leaves, so are some *Trouts* in some Rivers longer before they go out of season.

CHAP. IV.

And having told you these Observations concerning *Trouts*, I shall next tell you how to catch them: which is usually with a *Worm*, or a *Minnow* (which some call a *Penke*;) or with a *Flie*, either a *natural* or an *artificial* Flie: Concerning which three I wil give you some Observations and Directions.

For Worms, there be very many sorts; some bred onely in the earth, as the *earthworm*; others amongst or of plants, as the *dugworm*; and others in the bodies of living creatures; or some of dead flesh, as the *Magot* or *Gentle*, and others.

Now these be most of them particularly good for particular fishes: but for the *Trout* the *dew-worm*, (which some also cal the *Lob-worm*) and the *Brandling* are the chief; and especially the first for a great Trout, and the later for a lesse. There be also of *lob-worms*, some called *squirel-tails* (a worm which has a red head, a streak down the back, and a broad tail) which are noted to be the best, because they are the toughest, and most lively, and live longest in the water: for you are to know, that a dead worm is but a dead bait, and like to catch nothing, compared to a lively, quick, stirring worm: And for a *Brandling*, hee is usually found in an old dunghil, or some very rotten place neer to it; but most usually in cow dung, or hogs dung, rather than horse dung, which is somewhat too hot and dry for that worm.

There are also divers other kindes of worms, which for colour and shape alter even as the ground out of which they are got: as the *marsh-worm*, the *tag-tail*, the *flag-worm*, the *dock-worm*, the *oake-worm*, the *gilt-tail*, and too many to name, even as many sorts, as some think there be of severall kinds of birds in the air: of which I shall say no more, but tell you, that what worms soever you fish with, are the better for being long kept before they be used; and in case you have not been so provident, then the way to cleanse and scoure them quickly, is to put them all night in water, if they be Lob-worms, and then put them into your bag with fennel: but

you must not put your Brandling above an hour in water, and then put them into fennel for sudden use: but if you have time, and purpose to keep them long, then they be best preserved in an earthen pot with good store of *mosse*, which is to be fresh every week or
5 eight dayes; or at least taken from them, and clean wash'd, and wrung betwixt your hands till it be dry, and then put it to them again: And for Moss, you are to note, that there be divers kindes of it, which I could name to you, but wil onely tel you, that that which is likest a *Bucks horn* is the best; except it be *white* Moss, which
10 grows on some heaths, and is hard to be found.

For the *Minnow* or *Penke*, he is easily found and caught in April, for then hee appears in the Rivers: but Nature hath taught him to shelter and hide himself in the Winter in ditches that be neer to the River, and there both to hide and keep himself warm in
15 the weeds, which rot not so soon as in a running River; in which place if hee were in Winter, the distempered Floods that are usually in that season, would suffer him to have no rest, but carry him headlong to Mils and Weires to his confusion. And of these *Minnows*, first you are to know, that the biggest size is not the best: and next,
20 that the middle size and the whitest are the best: and then you are to know, that I cannot well teach in words, but must shew you how to put it on your hook, that it may turn the better: And you are also to know, that it is impossible it should turn too quick: And you are yet to know, that in case you want a Minnow, then a small
25 *Loch*, or a *Sticklebag*, or any other small Fish will serve as wel: And you are yet to know, that you may salt, and by that means keep them fit for use three or four dayes or longer; and that of salt, bay salt is the best.

Now for *Flies*, which is the third bait wherewith *Trouts* are usually
30 taken. You are to know, that there are as many sorts of Flies as there be of Fruits: I will name you but some of them: as the *dun flie*, the *stone flie*, the *red flie*, the *moor flie*, the *tawny flie*, the *shel flie*, the *cloudy* or blackish *flie*: there be of Flies, *Caterpillars*, and *Canker flies*, and *Bear flies*; and indeed, too many either for mee to name,
35 or for you to remember: and their breeding is so various and wonderful, that I might easily amaze my self, and tire you in a relation of them.

And yet I wil exercise your promised patience by saying a little of the *Caterpillar*, or the *Palmer flie* or *worm*; that by them you may guess what a work it were in a Discourse but to run over those very many *flies*, *worms*, and little living creatures with which the Sun and Summer adorn and beautifie the river banks and meadows; both for the recreation and contemplation of the Angler: and which (I think) I my self enjoy more then any other man that is not of my profession.

Pliny holds an opinion, that many have their birth or being from a dew that in the Spring falls upon the leaves of trees; and that some kinds of them are from a dew left upon herbs or flowers: and others from a dew left upon Colworts or Cabbages: All which kindes of dews being thickened and condensed, are by the Suns generative heat most of them hatch'd, and in three dayes made living creatures, and of several shapes and colours; some being hard and tough, some smooth and soft; some are horned in their head, some in their tail, some have none; some have hair, some none; some have sixteen feet, some less, and some have none: but (as our *Topsel* hath with † great diligence observed) those which have none, move upon the earth, or upon broad leaves, their motion being not unlike to the waves of the sea. Some of them hee also observes to be bred of the eggs of other Caterpillers: and that those in their time turn to be *Butter-flies*; and again, that their eggs turn the following yeer to be *Caterpillers*.

'Tis endlesse to tell you what the curious Searchers into Natures productions, have observed of these Worms and Flies: But yet I shall tell you what our *Topsel* sayes of the *Canker*, or *Palmer-worm*, or *Caterpiller*; That whereas others content themselves to feed on particular herbs or leaves (for most think, those very leaves that gave them life and shape, gives them a particular feeding and nourishment, and that upon them they usually abide;) yet he observes, that this is called a *Pilgrim* or *Palmer-worm*, for his very wandering life and various food; not contenting himself (as others do) with any certain place for his abode, nor any certain kinde of herb or flower for his feeding; but will boldly and disorderly

† *In his History of* Serpents.

wander up and down, and not endure to be kept to a diet, or fixt to a particular place.

Nay, the very colours of *Caterpillers* are, as one has observed, very elegant and beautiful: I shal (for a taste of the rest) describe one
5 of them, which I will sometime the next month, shew you feeding on a Willow tree, and you shal find him punctually to answer this very description: 'His lips and mouth somewhat yellow, his eyes black as Jet, his fore-head purple, his feet and hinder parts green, his tail two forked and black, the whole body stain'd with
10 a kind of red spots which run along the neck and shoulder-blades, not unlike the form of a Cross, or the letter X, made thus cross-wise, and a white line drawn down his back to his tail; all which add much beauty to his whole body.' And it is to me observable, that at a fix'd age this *Caterpiller* gives over to eat, and towards winter
15 comes to be cover'd over with a strange shell or crust, and so lives a kind of dead life, without eating all the winter, and (as others of several kinds turn to be several kinds of flies and vermin, the Spring
† following) so this *Caterpiller* then turns to be a painted Butterflye.

Come, come my Scholer, you see the River stops our morning
20 walk, and I wil also here stop my discourse, only as we sit down under this Honey-Suckle hedge, whilst I look a Line to fit the Rod that our brother *Peter* has lent you, I shall for a little confirmation of what I have said, repeat the observation of the Lord *Bartas*.

25
God not contented to each kind to give,
And to infuse the vertue generative,
By his wise power made many creatures breed
Of liveless bodies, without Venus *deed.*

So the cold humour breeds the Salamander,
Who (in effect) *like to her births commander,*
30
With child with hundred winters, with her touch
Quencheth the fire, though glowing ne'r so much

So in the fire in burning furnace springs
The Fly Perausta *with the flaming wings;*
Without the fire it dies, in it, it joyes,
35
Living in that which all things else destroyes.

† View Sir *Fra. Bacon* exper. 728 & 90. in his Natural History.

> *So slow* Boötes *underneath him sees*   †
> *In th'icie Islands* Goslings *hatcht of trees,*   ‡
> *Whose fruitful leaves falling into the water,*
> *Are turn'd ('tis known) to living fowls soon after*
>
> *So rotten planks of broken ships, do change*   5
> *To* Barnacles. *Oh transformation strange!*
> *'Twas first a green tree, then a broken hull,*
> *Lately a Mushroom, now a flying Gull.*

Viat. Oh my good Master, this morning walk has been spent to my great pleasure and wonder: but I pray, when shall I have your 10 direction how to make Artificial flyes, like to those that the *Trout* loves best? and also how to use them?

Pisc. My honest Scholer, it is now past five of the Clock, we will fish til nine, and then go to Breakfast: Go you to yonder *Sycamore tree*, and hide your bottle of drink under the hollow root of it; for 15 about that time, and in that place, we wil make a brave Breakfast with a piece of powdered Bief, and a Radish or two that I have in my Fish-bag; we shall, I warrant you, make a good honest, wholsome, hungry Breakfast, and I will give you direction for the making and using of your fly: and in the mean time, there is your 20 Rod and line; and my advice is, that you fish as you see mee do, and lets try which can catch the first fish.

Viat. I thank you, Master, I will observe and practice your direction as far as I am able.

Pisc. Look you Scholer, you see I have hold of a good fish: I 25 now see it is a *Trout*; I pray put that net under him, and touch not my line, for if you do, then wee break all. Well done, Scholer, I thank you. Now for an other. Trust me, I have another bite: Come Scholer, come lay down your Rod, and help me to land this as you did the other. So, now we shall be sure to have a good dish 30 of fish for supper.

Viat. I am glad of that, but I have no fortune; sure Master yours is a better Rod, and better Tackling.

† Gerh. Herbal.
‡ Cambden.

Pisc. Nay then, take mine and I will fish with yours. Look you, Scholer, I have another: come, do as you did before. And now I have a bite at another. Oh me he has broke all, there's half a line and a good hook lost.

5 *Viat.* Master, I can neither catch with the first nor second Angle; I have no fortune.

Pisc. Look you, Scholer, I have yet another: and now having caught three brace of *Trouts*, I will tel you a short Tale as we walk towards our Breakfast. A Scholer (a Preacher I should say) that was 10 to preach to procure the approbation of a Parish, that he might be their Lecturer, had got from a fellow Pupil of his the Copy of a Sermon that was first preached with a great commendation by him that composed and precht it; and though the borrower of it preach't it word for word, as it was at first, yet it was utterly dislik'd 15 as it was preach'd by the second; which the Sermon Borrower complained of to the Lender of it, and was thus answered; I lent you indeed my *Fiddle*, but not my *Fiddlestick*; and you are to know, that every one cannot make musick with my words which are fitted for my own mouth. And so my Scholer, you are to know, that as 20 the ill pronunciation or ill accenting of a word in a Sermon spoiles it, so the ill carriage of your Line, or not fishing even to a foot in a right place, makes you lose your labour: and you are to know, that though you have my Fiddle, that is, my very Rod and Tacklings with which you see I catch fish, yet you have not my Fiddle 25 stick, that is, skill to know how to carry your hand and line; and this must be taught you (for you are to remember I told you Angling is an Art) either by practice, or a long observation, or both.

But now lets say Grace, and fall to Breakfast; what say you 30 Scholer, to the providence of an old Angler? Does not this meat taste well? and was not this place well chosen to eat it? for this *Sycamore* tree will shade us from the Suns heat.

Viat. All excellent good, Master, and my stomack excellent too; I have been at many costly Dinners that have not afforded me half 35 this content: and now good Master, to your promised direction for making and ordering my Artificiall flye.

Pisc. My honest Scholer, I will do it, for it is a debt unto you,

by my promise: and because you shall not think your self more
engaged to me then indeed you really are, therefore I will tell you
freely, I find Mr *Thomas Barker* (a Gentleman that has spent much
time and money in Angling) deal so judicially and freely in a little
book of his of Angling, and especially of making and Angling with 5
a *flye* for a *Trout*, that I will give you his very directions without
much variation, which shal follow.

Let your rod be light, and very gentle, I think the best are of
two pieces; the line should not exceed, (especially for three or four
links towards the hook) I say, nòt exceed three or four haires; but 10
if you can attain to Angle with one haire, you will have more rises,
and catch more fish. Now you must bee sure not to cumber your
selfe with too long a Line, as most do: and before you begin to
angle, cast to have the wind on your back, and the sun (if it shines)
to be before you, and to fish down the streame; and carry the point 15
or top of the Rod downeward; by which meanes the shadow of
your selfe, and Rod too will be the least offensive to the Fish, for
the sight of any shadow amazes the fish, and spoiles your sport,
of which you must take a great care.

In the middle of *March* (till which time a man should not in 20
honestie catch a *Trout*) or in *April*, if the weather be dark, or a
little windy, or cloudie, the best fishing is with the *Palmer-worm*,
of which I last spoke to you; but of these there be divers kinds,
or at least of divers colours, these and the *May-fly* are the ground
of all *fly*-Angling, which are to be thus made: 25

First you must arm your hook, with the line in the inside of it;
then take your Scissers and cut so much of a browne *Malards* feather
as in your own reason will make the wings of it, you having withall
regard to the bigness or littleness of your hook, then lay the outmost
part of your feather next to your hook, then the point of your feather 30
next the shank of your hook; and having so done, whip it three
or four times about the hook with the same Silk, with which your
hook was armed, and having made the Silk fast, take the hackel
of a *Cock* or *Capons* neck, or a *Plovers* top, which is usually better;
take off the one side of the feather, and then take the hackel, Silk 35
or Crewel, Gold or Silver thred, make these fast at the bent of
the hook, that is to say, below your arming, then you must take

the hackel, the silver or gold thred, and work it up to the wings, shifting or stil removing your fingers as you turn the Silk about the hook: and still looking at every stop or turne that your gold, or what materials soever you make your *Fly* of, do lye right and
5 neatly; and if you find they do so, then when you have made the head, make all fast, and then work your hackel up to the head, and make that fast; and then with a needle or pin divide the wing into two, and then with the arming Silk whip it about cross-wayes betwixt the wings, and then with your thumb you must turn the
10 point of the feather towards the bent of the hook, and then work three or four about the shank of the hook, and then view the proportion, and if all be neat, and to your liking, fasten.

I confess, no direction can be given to make a man of a dull capacity able to make a flye well; and yet I know, this, with a little
15 practice, wil help an ingenuous Angler in a good degree; but to see a fly made by another, is the best teaching to make it, and then an ingenuous Angler may walk by the River and mark what fly falls on the water that day, and catch one of them if he see the *Trouts* leap at a fly of that kind, and having alwaies hooks ready hung
20 with him, and having a bag also, alwaies with him with Bears hair, or the hair of a brown or sad coloured Heifer, hackels of a Cock or Capon, several coloured Silk and Crewel to make the body of the fly, the feathers of a Drakes head, black or brown sheeps wool, or Hogs wool, or hair, thred of Gold, and of silver; silk of several
25 colours (especially sad coloured to make the head;) and there be also other colour'd feathers both of birds and of peckled fowl. I say, having those with him in a bag, and trying to make a flie, though he miss at first, yet shal he at last hit it better, even to a perfection which none can well teach him; and if he hit to make
30 his *flie* right, and have the luck to hit also where there is store of *trouts*, and a right wind, he shall catch such store of them, as will encourage him to grow more and more in love with the Art of *flie-making*.

Viat. But my loving Master, if any wind will not serve, then I
35 wish I were in *Lapland*, to buy a good wind of one of the honest witches that sell so many winds, and so cheap.

Pisc. Marry Scholer, but I would not be there, nor indeed from under this tree; for look how it begins to rain, and by the clouds (if I mistake not) we shall presently have a smoaking showre; and therefore sit close, this *Sycamore* tree will shelter us; and I will tell you, as they shall come into my mind, more observations of flie-fishing for a *Trout*.   5

But first, for the winde; you are to take notice that of the windes the *South winde* is said to be best. One observes, That

> *When the winde is south,*
> *It blows your bait into a fishes mouth.*

Next to that, the *west* winde is believed to be the best: and having   10
told you that the *East* winde is the worst, I need not tell you which winde is best in the third degree: And yet (as *Solomon* observes,) that *Hee that considers the winde shall never sow*: so hee that busies his head too much about them, (if the weather be not made extreme cold by an East winde) shall be a little superstitious: for as it is   15
observed by some, That there is no good horse of a bad colour; so I have observed, that if it be a clowdy day, and not extreme cold, let the winde sit in what corner it will, and do its worst. And yet take this for a Rule, that I would willingly fish on the Lee-shore: and you are to take notice, that the Fish lies, or swimms neerer   20
the bottom in Winter then in Summer, and also neerer the bottom in any cold day.

But I promised to tell you more of the Flie-fishing for a *Trout*, (which I may have time enough to do, for you see it rains *May-butter*.) First, for a *May-flie*, you may make his body with greenish   25
coloured crewel, or willow colour; darkning it in most places, with waxed silk, or ribd with a black hare, or some of them rib'd with silver thred; and such wings for the colour as you see the flie to have at that season; nay at that very day on the water. Or you may make the *Oak-flie* with an Orange-tawny and black ground, and the   30
brown of a Mallards feather for the wings; and you are to know, that these two are most excellent *flies*, that is, the *May flie* and the *Oak-flie*: And let me again tell you, that you keep as far from the water as you can possibly, whether you fish with a flie or worm, and fish down the stream; and when you fish with a flie,   35
if it be possible, let no part of your line touch the water, but your

flie only; and be stil moving your fly upon the water, or casting it into the water; you your self, being also alwaies moving down the stream. Mr *Barker* commends severall sorts of the palmer flies, not only those rib'd with silver and gold, but others that have
5 their bodies all made of black, or some with red, and a red hackel; you may also make the *hawthorn-flie*, which is all black and not big, but very smal, the smaller the better; or the *oak-fly*, the body of which is Orange colour and black of crewel, with a brown wing, or a *fly* made with a peacocks feather, is excellent in a bright day:
10 you must be sure you want not in your *Magazin* bag, the Peacocks feather, and grounds of such wool, and crewel as will make the Grasshopper: and note, that usually, the smallest flies are best; and note also, that, the light flie does usually make most sport in a dark day: and the darkest and least flie in a bright or cleare day;
15 and lastly note, that you are to repair upon any occasion to your *Magazin bag*, and upon any occasion vary and make them according to your fancy.

And now I shall tell you, that the fishing with a natural flie is excellent, and affords much pleasure; they may be found thus, the
20 *May-fly* usually in and about that month neer to the River side, especially against rain; the *Oak-fly* on the Butt or body of an *Oak* or *Ash*, from the beginning of *May* to the end of *August*; it is a brownish fly, and easie to be so found, and stands usually with his head downward, that is to say, towards the root of the tree; the
25 smal black fly, or *hawthorn* fly is to be had on any Hawthorn bush, after the leaves be come forth; with these and a short Line (as I shewed to Angle for a *Chub*) you may dap or drop, and also with a *Grashopper*, behind a tree, or in any deep hole, still making it to move on the top of the water, as if it were alive, and still keeping
30 yourself out of sight, you shall certainly have sport if there be *Trouts*; yea in a hot day, but especially in the evening of a hot day.

And now, Scholer, my direction for fly-fishing is ended with this showre, for it has done raining, and now look about you, and see how pleasantly that Meadow looks, nay and the earth smels as
35 sweetly too. Come let me tell you what holy Mr *Herbert* saies of such dayes and Flowers as these, and then we will thank God that

we enjoy them, and walk to the River and sit down quietly and
try to catch the other brace of *Trouts*.

> *Sweet day, so cool, so calm, so bright,*
> *The bridal of the earth and skie,*
> *Sweet dews shal weep thy fall to night,*
> > *for thou must die.*   5
>
> *Sweet Rose, whose hew angry and brave*
> *Bids the rash gazer wipe his eye,*
> *Thy root is ever in its grave,*
> > *and thou must die.*   10
>
> *Sweet Spring, ful of sweet dayes and roses,*
> *A box where sweets compacted lie;*
> *My Musick shewes you have your closes,*
> > *and all must die.*
>
> *Only a sweet and vertuous soul,*   15
> *Like seasoned timber never gives,*
> *But when the whole world turns to cole,*
> > *then chiefly lives.*

Viat. I thank you, good Master, for your good direction for fly-
fishing, and for the sweet enjoyment of the pleasant day, which is   20
so far spent without offence to God or man: and I thank you for
the sweet close of your discourse with Mr *Herberts* Verses, which I
have heard, loved Angling; and I do the rather believe it, because
he had a spirit sutable to Anglers, and to the those Primitive Christians that you love, and have so much commended.   25

Pisc. Well, my loving Scholer, and I am pleased to know that
you are so well pleased with my direction and discourse; and I hope
you will be pleased too, if you find a *Trout* at one of our Angles,
which we left in the water to fish for it self; you shall chuse which
shall be yours, and it is an even lay, one catches: And let me tell   30
you, this kind of fishing, and laying Night-hooks, are like putting
money to use, for they both work for the Owners, when they do
nothing but sleep, or eat, or rejoice, as you know we have done
this last hour, and sate as quietly and as free from cares under this
Sycamore, as *Virgils Tityrus* and his *Meliboeus* did under their broad   35

Beech tree: No life, my honest Scholer, no life so happy and so pleasant as the Anglers, unless it be the Beggers life in Summer; for then only they take no care, but are as happy as we Anglers.

Viat. Indeed Master, and so they be, as is witnessed by the beggers Song, made long since by *Frank Davison*, a good Poet, who was not a Begger, though he were a good Poet.

Pisc. Can you sing it, Scholer?

Viat. Sit down a little, good Master, and I wil try.

> *Bright shines the Sun, play beggers, play,*
> *here's scraps enough to serve to day:*
> *What noise of viols is so sweet*
> *As when our merry clappers ring?*
> *What mirth doth want when beggers meet?*
> *A beggers life is for a King:*
> *Eat, drink and play, sleep when we list,*
> *Go where we will so stocks be mist.*
> *Bright shines the Sun, play beggers, &c.*

> *The world is ours and ours alone,*
> *For we alone have world at will;*
> *We purchase not, all is our own,*
> *Both fields and streets we beggers fill,*
> *Play beggers play, play beggers play,*
> *here's scraps enough to serve to day.*

> *A hundred herds of black and white*
> *Upon our Gowns securely feed,*
> *And yet if any dare us bite,*
> *He dies therefore as sure as Creed:*
> *Thus beggers Lord it as they please,*
> *And only beggers live at ease:*
> *Bright shines the Sun, play beggers play,*
> *here's scraps enough to serve to day.*

Pisc. I thank you good Scholer, this Song was well humor'd by the maker, and well remembered and sung by you; and I pray forget not the Ketch which you promised to make against night, for our Country man honest *Coridon* will expect your Ketch and my Song, which I must be forc'd to patch up, for it is so long since I learnt it, that I have forgot a part of it. But come, lets stretch our legs a little in a gentle walk to the River, and try what interest our Angles wil pay us for lending them so long to be used by the *Trouts*.

Viat. Oh me, look you Master, a fish, a fish.

Pisc. I marry Sir, that was a good fish indeed; if I had had the luck to have taken up that Rod, 'tis twenty to one he should not 5 have broke my line by running to the Rods end, as you suffered him; I would have held him, unless he had been fellow to the great *Trout* that is neer an ell long, which had his picture drawne, and now to be seen at mine Hoste *Rickabies* at the *George* in *Ware*; and it may be, by giving that *Trout* the Rod, that is, by casting it to 10 him into the water, I might have caught him at the long run, for so I use alwaies to do when I meet with an over-grown fish, and you will learn to do so hereafter; for I tell you, Scholer, fishing is an Art, or at least, it is an Art to catch fish.

Viat. But, Master, will this *Trout* die, for it is like he has the hook 15 in his belly?

Pisc. I wil tel you, Scholer, that unless the hook be fast in his very Gorge, he wil live, and a little time with the help of the water, wil rust the hook, and it wil in time wear away as the gravel does in the horse hoof, which only leaves a false quarter. 20

And now Scholer, lets go to my Rod. Look you Scholer, I have a fish too, but it proves a logger-headed *Chub*; and this is not much a miss, for this wil pleasure some poor body, as we go to our lodging to meet our brother *Peter* and honest *Coridon*. Come, now bait your hook again, and lay it into the water, for it rains again, and we 25 wil ev'n retire to the *Sycamore* tree, and there I wil give you more directions concerning fishing; for I would fain make you an Artist.

Viat. Yes, good Master, I pray let it be so.

CHAP. V.

Pisc. Wel, Scholer, now we are sate downe and are at ease, I shall tel you a little more of *Trout* fishing before I speak of the *Salmon*, (which I purpose shall be next) and then of the *Pike* or *Luce*. You 5 are to know, there is night as well as day-fishing for a *Trout*, and that then the best are out of their holds; and the manner of taking them is on the top of the water with a great *Lob* or *Garden worm*, or rather two; which you are to fish for in a place where the water runs somewhat quietly (for in a stream it wil not be so well 10 discerned.) I say, in a quiet or dead place neer to some swift, there draw your bait over the top of the water to and fro, and if there be a good *Trout* in the hole, he wil take it, especially if the night be dark; for then he lies boldly neer the top of the water, watching the motion of any *Frog* or *Water-mouse*, or *Rat* betwixt him and the 15 skie, which he hunts for if he sees the water but wrinkle or move in one of these dead holes, where the great *Trouts* usually lye neer to their hold.

And you must fish for him with a strong line, and not a little hook, and let him have time to gorge your hook, for he does not 20 usually forsake it, as he oft will in the day-fishing: and if the night be not dark, then fish so with an *Artificial fly* of a light colour; nay he will sometimes rise at a dead *Mouse* or a piece of cloth, or any thing that seemes to swim cross the water, or to be in motion: this is a choice way, but I have not oft used it because it is void of 25 the pleasures that such dayes as these that we now injoy, afford an *Angler*.

And you are to know, that in *Hamp-shire*, (which I think exceeds all *England* for pleasant Brooks, and store of *Trouts*) they use to catch *Trouts* in the night by the light of a Torch or straw, which when 30 they have discovered, they strike with a *Trout* spear; this kind of way they catch many, but I would not believe it till I was an eye-witness of it, nor like it now I have seen it.

Viat. But Master, do not *Trouts* see us in the night?

74

Pisc. Yes, and hear, and smel too, both then and in the day time, for *Gesner* observes, the *Otter* smels a fish forty furlong off him in the water; and that it may be true, is affirmed by Sir *Francis Bacon* (in the eighth Century of his Natural History) who there proves, that waters may be the *Medium* of sounds, by demonstrating it thus, *That if you knock two stones together very deep under the water, those that stand on a bank neer to that place may hear the noise without any diminution of it by the water.* He also offers the like experiment concerning the letting an *Anchor* fall by a very long Cable or rope on a Rock, or the sand within the Sea: and this being so well observed and demonstrated, as it is by that learned man, has made me to believe that Eeles unbed themselves, and stir at the noise of the Thunder, and not only as some think, by the motion or the stirring of the earth, which is occasioned by that Thunder.

And this reason of Sir *Francis Bacons* has made me crave pardon † 15 of one that I laugh at, for affirming that he knew *Carps* come to a certain place in a Pond to be fed at the ringing of a Bel; and it shall be a rule for me to make as little noise as I can when I am a fishing, until Sir *Francis Bacon* be confuted, which I shal give any man leave to do, and so leave off this Philosophical discourse 20 for a discourse of fishing.

Of which my next shall be to tell you, it is certain, that certain fields neer *Lemster*, a Town in *Hereford-shire*, are observed, that they make the Sheep that graze upon them more fat then the next, and also to bear finer Wool; that is to say, that that year in which they 25 feed in such a particular pasture, they shall yeeld finer wool then the yeer before they came to feed in it, and courser again if they shall return to their former pasture, and again return to a finer wool being fed in the fine wool ground. Which I tell you, that you may the better believe that I am certain, If I catch a *Trout* in one 30 Meadow, he shall be *white* and *faint*, and very like to be *lowsie*; and as certainly if I catch a *Trout* in the next Meadow, he shal be *strong*, and *red*, and *lusty*, and much better meat: Trust me (Scholer) I have caught many a *Trout* in a particular Meadow, that the very shape and inamelled colour of him, has joyed me to look upon him, 35

† *Exper.* 792

5

10

and I have with *Solomon* concluded, *Every thing is beautifull in his season.*

It is now time to tell you next, (according to promise) some observations of the *Salmon*; But first, I wil tel you there is a fish, called by some an *Umber*, and by some a *Greyling*, a choice fish, 5 esteemed by many to be equally good with the *Trout*: it is a fish that is usually about eighteen inches long, he lives in such streams as the *Trout* does; and is indeed taken with the same bait as a *Trout* is, for he will bite both at the *Minnow*, the *Worm*, and the *Fly*, both *Natural* and *Artificial*: of this fish there be many in *Trent*, and in 10 the River that runs by *Salisbury*, and in some other lesser Brooks; but he is not so general a fish as the *Trout*, nor to me either so good to eat, or so pleasant to fish for as the *Trout* is; of which two fishes I will now take my leave, and come to my promised Observations of the *Salmon*, and a little advice for the catching him.

CHAP. VI.

The *Salmon* is ever bred in the fresh Rivers (and in most Rivers about the month of *August*) and never grows big but in the *Sea*; and there to an incredible bigness in a very short time; to which place they covet to swim, by the instinct of nature, about a set 5 time: but if they be stopp'd by *Mills*, *Floud-gates* or *Weirs*, or be by accident lost in the fresh water, when the others go (which is usually by flocks or sholes) then they thrive not.

And the old *Salmon*, both the *Melter* and *Spawner*, strive also to get into the *Sea* before Winter; but being stopt that course, or lost, 10 grow sick in fresh waters, and by degrees unseasonable, and kipper, that is, to have a bony gristle, to grow (not unlike a *Hauks* beak) on one of this chaps, which hinders him from feeding, and then he pines and dies.

But if he gets to *Sea*, then that gristle wears away, or is cast off 15 (as the *Eagle* is said to cast his bill) and he recovers his strength, and comes next Summer to the same river, (if it be possible) to enjoy the former pleasures that there possest him; for (as one has wittily observed) he has (like some persons of Honour and Riches, which have both their winter and Summer houses) the fresh Rivers 20 for Summer, and the salt water for winter to spend his life in; which is not (as Sir *Francis Bacon* hath observed) above ten years: And †it is to be observed, that though they grow big in the *Sea*, yet they grow not fat but in fresh Rivers; and it is observed, that the farther they get from the *Sea*, the better they be. 25

And it is observed, that, to the end they may get far from the *Sea*, either to Spawne or to possess the pleasure that they then and there find, they will force themselves over the tops of *Weirs*, or *Hedges*, or *stops* in the water, by taking their tails into their mouthes, and leaping over those places, even to a height beyond common 30 belief: and sometimes by forcing themselves against the streame

† In his History of Life and Death.

through Sluces and Floud-gates, beyond common credit. And 'tis observed by *Gesner*, that there is none bigger then in *England*, nor none better then in Thames.

And for the *Salmons* sudden growth, it has been observed by tying
5 a Ribon in the tail of some number of the young *Salmons*, which have been taken in *Weires*, as they swimm'd towards the salt water, and then by taking a part of them again with the same mark, at the same place, at their returne from the Sea, which is usually about six months after; and the like experiment hath been tried upon
10 young *Swallows*, who have after six months absence, been observed to return to the same chimney, there to make their nests, and their habitations for the Summer following; which hath inclined many to think, that every *Salmon* usually returns to the same river in which it was bred, as young *Pigeons* taken out of the same *Dove-cote*, have
15 also been observed to do.

And you are yet to observe further, that the He *Salmon* is usually bigger then the Spawner, and that he is more kipper, and less able to endure a winter in the fresh water, then the She is; yet she is at that time of looking less kipper and better, as watry and as bad
20 meat.

And yet you are to observe, that as there is no general rule without an exception, so there is some few Rivers in this Nation that have *Trouts* and *Salmon* in season in winter. But for the observations of that and many other things, I must in manners omit, because they
25 wil prove too large for our narrow compass of time, and therefore I shall next fall upon my direction how to fish for the *Salmon*.

And for that, first, you shall observe, that usually he staies not long in a place (as *Trouts* wil) but (as I said) covets still to go neerer the Spring head; and he does not (as the *Trout* and many other
30 fish) lie neer the water side or bank, or roots of trees, but swims usually in the middle, and neer the ground; and that there you are to fish for him; and that he is to be caught as the *Trout* is, with a *Worm*, a *Minnow*, (which some call a *Penke*) or with a *Fly*.

And you are to observe, that he is very, very seldom observed
35 to bite at a *Minnow* (yet sometime he will) and not oft at a *fly*, but more usually at a *Worm*, and then most usually at a *Lob* or *Garden worm*, which should be wel scowred, that is to say, seven

or eight dayes in Moss before you fish with them; and if you double
your time of eight into sixteen, or more, into twenty or more days,
it is still the better, for the worms will stil be clearer, tougher, and
more lively, and continue so longer upon your hook.

And now I shall tell you, that which may be called a secret: I
have been a fishing with old *Oliver Henly* (now with God) a noted
Fisher, both for *Trout* and *Salmon*, and have observed that he would
usually take three or four worms out of his bag and put them into
a little box in his pocket, where he would usually let them continue
half an hour or more, before he would bait his hook with them;
I have ask'd him his reason, and he has replied, *He did but pick
the best out to be in a readiness against he baited his hook the next time*:
But he has been observed both by others, and my self, to catch
more fish then I or any other body, that has ever gone a fishing
with him, could do, especially *Salmons*; and I have been told lately
by one of his most intimate and secret friends, that the box in which
he put those worms was anointed with a drop, or two, or three
of the Oil of *Ivy-berries*, made by expression or infusion, and that
by the wormes remaining in that box an hour, or a like time, they
had incorporated a kind of smel that was irresistibly attractive,
enough to force any fish, within the smel of them, to bite. This
I heard not long since from a friend, but have not tryed it; yet
I grant it probable, and refer my Reader to Sir *Francis Bacons*
Natural History, where he proves fishes may hear; and I am certain
Gesner sayes, the *Otter* can smell in the water, and know not but
that fish may do so too: 'tis left for a lover of Angling, or any that
desires to improve that Art, to try this conclusion.

I shall also impart another experiment (but not tryed by my selfe)
which I wil deliver in the same words as it was by a friend, given
me in writing.

Take the stinking oil drawn out of Polypody *of the Oak, by a retort
mixt with* Turpentine, *and Hive-honey, and annoint your bait therewith, and
it will doubtless draw the fish to it.*

But in these things I have no great faith, yet grant it probable,
and have had from some chimical men (namely, from Sir *George
Hastings* and others) an affirmation of them to be very advantage-
ous: but no more of these, especially not in this place.

I might here, before I take my leave of the *Salmon*, tell you, that there is more then one sort of them, as namely, a *Tecon*, and another called in some places a *Samlet*, or by some, a *Skegger*: but these (and others which I forbear to name) may be fish of another kind, and differ, as we know a *Herring* and a *Pilcher* do; but must by me be left to the disquisitions of men of more leisure and of greater abilities, then I profess my self to have.

And lastly, I am to borrow so much of your promised patience, as to tell you, that the *Trout* or *Salmon*, being in season, have at their first taking out of the water (which continues during life) their bodies adorned, the one with such red spots, and the other with black or blackish spots, which gives them such an addition of natural beautie, as I (that yet am no enemy to it) think was never given to any woman by the Artificial Paint or Patches in which they so much pride themselves in this age. And so I shall leáve them and proceed to some Observations of the *Pike*.

CHAP. VII.

Pisc. It is not to be doubted but that the *Luce*, or *Pikrell*, or *Pike* breeds by Spawning; and yet *Gesner* sayes, that some of them breed, where none ever was, out of a weed called *Pikrell*-weed, and other glutinous matter, which with the help of the suns heat proves in 5 some particular ponds (apted by nature for it) to become *Pikes*.

Sir *Francis Bacon* observes the *Pike* to be the longest lived of any † fresh water fish, and yet that his life is not usually above fortie years; and yet *Gesner* mentions a *Pike* taken in *Swedeland* in the year 1449, with a Ring about his neck, declaring he was put into the 10 Pond by *Frederick* the second, more then two hundred years before he was last taken, as the Inscription of that Ring, being Greek, was interpreted by the then Bishop of *Worms*. But of this no more, but that it is observed that the old or very great *Pikes* have in them more of state then goodness; the smaller or middle siz'd *Pikes* being 15 by the most and choicest palates observed to be the best meat; but contrary, the Eele is observed to be the better for age and bigness.

All *Pikes* that live long prove chargeable to their keepers, because their life is maintained by the death of so many other fish, even those of his owne kind, which has made him by some Writers to 20 bee called the *Tyrant* of the Rivers, or the *Freshwater-wolf*, by reason of his bold, greedy, devouring disposition; which is so keen, as *Gesner* relates, a man going to a Pond (where it seems a *Pike* had devoured all the fish) to water his Mule, had a *Pike* bit his Mule by the lips, to which the *Pike* hung so fast, that the *Mule* drew him out of the 25 water, and by that accident the owner of the *Mule* got the *Pike*; I tell you who relates it, and shall with it tel you what a wise man has observed, *It is a hard thing to perswade the belly, because it hath no ears.*

But if this relation of *Gesners* bee dis-believed, it is too evident 30 to bee doubted that a *Pike* will devoure a fish of his own kind, that

† In his History of Life and Death.

shall be bigger then his belly or throat will receive; and swallow a part of him, and let the other part remain in his mouth till the swallowed part be digested, and then swallow that other part that was in his mouth, and so put it over by degrees. And it is observed,
5 that the *Pike* will eat venemous things (as some kinds of *Frogs* are) and yet live without being harmed by them: for, as some say, he has in him a natural Balsome or Antidote against all Poison: and others, that he never eats a venemous *Frog* till he hath first killed her, and then (as *Ducks* are observed to do to *Frogs* in Spawning
10 time, at which time some *Frogs* are observed to be venemous) so throughly washt her, by tumbling her up and down in the water, that he may devour her without danger. And *Gesner* affirms, that a *Polonian* Gentleman did faithfully assure him, he had seen two young Geese at one time in the belly of a *Pike*: and hee observes, that
15 in *Spain* there is no *Pikes*, and that the biggest are in the Lake *Thracimane* in *Italy*, and the next, if not equal to them, are the *Pikes* of *England*.

The *Pike* is also observed to be a melancholy, and a bold fish: Melancholy, because he alwaies swims or rests himselfe alone, and
20 never swims in sholes, or with company, as *Roach*, and *Dace*, and most other fish do: And bold, because he fears not a shadow, or to see or be seen of any body, as the *Trout* and *Chub*, and all other fish do.

And it is observed by *Gesner*, that the bones, and hearts, and gals
25 of *Pikes* are very medicinable for several Diseases, as to stop bloud, to abate Fevers, to cure Agues, to oppose or expel the infection of the Plague, and to be many wayes medicinable and useful for the good of mankind; but that the biting of a *Pike* is venemous and hard to be cured.

30 And it is observed, that the *Pike* is a fish that breeds but once a year, and that other fish (as namely *Leaches*) do breed oftner; as we are certaine Pigeons do almost every month, and yet the Hawk, a bird of prey (as the *Pike* is of fish) breeds but once in twelve months: and you are to note, that his time of breeding or Spawning
35 is usually about the end of *February*; or somewhat later, in *March*, as the weather proves colder or warmer: and to note, that his manner of breeding is thus, a He and a She *Pike* will usually go together

out of a River into some ditch or creek, and that there the Spawner casts her eggs, and the Melter hovers over her all that time that she is casting her Spawn, but touches her not. I might say more of this, but it might be thought curiosity or worse, and shall therefore, forbear it, and take up so much of your attention to tell you, that 5 the best of *Pikes* are noted to be in Rivers, then those in great Ponds or Meres, and the worst in smal Ponds.

And now I shall proceed to give you some direction how to catch this *Pike*, which you have with so much patience heard me talk of.   10

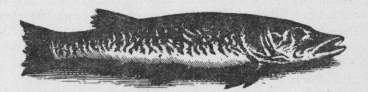

His feeding is usually *fish* or *frogs*, and sometime a weed of his owne, called *Pikrel-weed*, of which I told you some think some *Pikes* are bred; for they have observed, that where no *Pikes* have been put into a Pond, yet that there they have been found, and that there has been plenty of that weed in that Pond, and that that weed 15 both breeds and feeds them; but whether those *Pikes* so bred will ever breed by generation as the others do, I shall leave to the disquisitions of men of more curiosity and leisure then I profess my self to have; and shall proceed to tell you, that you may fish for a *Pike*, either with a ledger, or a walking bait; and you are to note, 20 that I call that a ledger which is fix'd, or made to rest in one certaine place when you shall be absent; and that I call that a walking bait, which you take with you, and have ever in motion. Concerning which two, I shall give you this direction, That your ledger bait is best to be a living bait, whether it be a fish or a Frog; and that 25 you may make them live the longer, you may, or indeed you must take this course:

First, for your live bait of fish, a *Roch* or *Dace* is (I think) best

and most tempting, and a *Pearch* the longest liv'd on a hook; you must take your knife, (which cannot be too sharp) and betwixt the head and the fin on his back, cut or make an insition, or such a scar as you may put the arming wyer of your hook into it, with
5 as little bruising or hurting the fish as Art and diligence will enable you to do, and so carrying your arming wyer along his back, unto, or neer the tail of your fish, betwixt the skin and the body of it, draw out that wyer or arming of your hook at another scar neer to his tail; then tye him about it with thred, but no harder then
10 of necessitie you must to prevent hurting the fish; and the better to avoid hurting the fish, some have a kind of probe to open the way, for the more easie entrance and passage of your wyer or arm-ing: but as for these, time and a little experience will teach you better then I can by words; for of this I will for the present say no
15 more, but come next to give you some directions how to bait your hook with a Frog.

Viat. But, good Master, did not you say even now, that some *Frogs* were venemous, and is it not dangerous to touch them?

Pisc. Yes, but I wil give you some Rules or Cautions concerning
20 them: And first, you are to note, there is two kinds of *Frogs*; that is to say, (if I may so express my self) a *flesh* and a *fish-frog*: by flesh *Frogs*, I mean, *frogs* that breed and live on the land; and of these there be several sorts and colours, some being peckled, some greenish, some blackish, or brown: the green *Frog*, which is a smal
25 one, is by *Topsell* taken to be venemous; and so is the *Padock*, or *Frog-Padock*, which usually keeps or breeds on the land, and is very large and bony, and big, especially the She *frog* of that kind; yet these will sometime come into the water, but it is not often; and the land *frogs* are some of them observed by him, to breed by laying
30 eggs, and others to breed of the slime and dust of the earth, and that in winter they turn to slime again, and that the next Summer that very slime returns to be a living creature; this is the opinion of *Pliny*; and *Cardanas* undertakes to give reason for the raining of *Frogs*; but if it were in my power, it should rain none but water

† *Topsel* of *Frogs*.
* In his 16th Book, *De subtil. ex.*

Frogs, for those I think are not venemous, especially the right water *Frog*, which about *February* or *March* breeds in ditches by slime and blackish eggs in that slime, about which time of breeding the He and She *frog* are observed to use divers simber salts, and to croke and make a noise, which the land *frog*, or *Padock frog* never does. 5 Now of these water *Frogs*, you are to chuse the yellowest that you can get, for that the *Pike* ever likes best. And thus use your *Frog*, that he may continue long alive:

Put your hook into his mouth, which you may easily do from about the middle of *April* till *August*, and then the *Frogs* mouth grows 10 up and he continues so for at least six months without eating, but is sustained, none, but he whose name is wonderful, knows how. I say, put your hook, I mean the arming wire, through his mouth and out at his gills, and then with a fine needle and Silk sow the upper part of his leg with only one stitch to the armed wire of your 15 hook, or tie the *frogs* leg above the upper joint to the armed wire, and in so doing use him as though you loved him, that is, harme him as little as you may possibly, that he may live the longer.

And now, having given you this direction for the baiting your ledger hook with a live fish or frog, my next must be to tell you, 20 how your hook thus baited must or may be used; and it is thus: Having fastned your hook to a line, which if it be not fourteen yards long, should not be less then twelve; you are to fasten that line to any bow neer to a hole where a *Pike* is, or is likely to lye, or to have a haunt, and then wind your line on any forked stick, 25 all your line, except a half yard of it, or rather more, and split that forked stick with such a nick or notch at one end of it, as may keep the line from any more of it ravelling from about the stick, then so much of it as you intended; and chuse your forked stick to be of that bigness as may keep the *fish* or *frog* from pulling the 30 forked stick under the water till the *Pike* bites, and then the *Pike* having pulled the line forth of the clift or nick in which it was gently fastned, will have line enough to go to his hold and powch the bait: and if you would have this ledger bait to keep at a fixt place, undisturbed by wind or other accidents, which may drive it to the 35 shoare side (for you are to note that it is likeliest to catch a *Pike*

in the midst of the water) then hang a small Plummet of lead, a stone, or piece of tyle, or a turfe in a string, and cast it into the water, with the forked stick to hang upon the ground, to be as an Anchor to keep the forked stick from moving out of your intended
5 place till the *Pike* come. This I take to be a very good way, to use so many ledger baits as you intend to make tryal of.

Or if you bait your hooks thus, with live fish or Frogs, and in a windy day fasten them thus to a bow or bundle of straw, and by the help of that wind can get them to move cross a *Pond* or
10 *Mere*, you are like to stand still on the shoar and see sport, if there by any store of *Pikes*; or these live baits may make sport, being tied about the body or wings of a *Goose* or *Duck*, and she chased over a Pond: and the like may be done with turning three or four live baits thus fastned to bladders, or boughs, or bottles of hay, or flags,
15 to swim down a *River*, whilst you walk quietly on the shore along with them, and are still in expectation of sport. The rest must be taught you by practice, for time will not alow me to say more of this kind of fishing with live baits.

And for your dead bait for a *Pike*, for that you may be taught
20 by one dayes going a fishing with me or any other body that fishes for him, for the baiting of your hook with a dead *Gudgion* or a *Roach*, and moving it up and down the water, is too easie a thing to take up any time to direct you to do it; and yet, because I cut you short in that, I will commute for it, by telling you that that was told
25 me for a secret: it is this:

Dissolve Gum of Ivie *in Oyle of* Spike, *and therewith annoint your dead bait for a* Pike, *and then cast it into a likely place, and when it has layen a short time at the bottom, draw it towards the top of the water, and so up the stream, and it is more then likely that you have a* Pike *follow you*
30 *with more then common eagerness.*

This has not been tryed by me, but told me by a friend of note, that pretended to do me a courtesie: but if this direction to catch a Pike thus do you no good, I am certaine this direction how to roste him when he is caught, is choicely good, for I have tryed it,
35 and it is somewhat the better for not being common; but with my direction you must take this Caution, that your Pike must not be a smal one.

First open your Pike *at the gills, and if need be, cut also a little slit*
towards his belly; out of these, take his guts, and keep his liver, which you
are to shred very small with Time, Sweet Margerom, *and a little*
Winter-Savoury; *to these put some pickled* Oysters, *and some* Anchovis,
both these last whole (for the Anchovis *will melt, and the* Oysters *should* 5
not:) to these you must add also a pound of sweet Butter, which you are to
mix with the herbs that are shred, and let them all be well salted (if the Pike
be more then a yard long, then you may put into these herbs more then a pound,
or if he be less, then less Butter will suffice:) these being mixt, with a blade
or two of Mace, *must be put into the* Pikes *belly, and then his belly sowed* 10
up; then you are to thrust the spit through his mouth out at his tail; and then
with four, or five, or six split sticks or very thin laths, and a convenient
quantitie of tape or filiting, these laths are to be tyed round about the Pikes
body, from his head to his tail, and the tape tied somewhat thick to prevent his
breaking or falling off from the spit; let him be rosted very leisurely, and often 15
basted with Claret *wine, and* Anchovis, *and butter mixt together, and also*
with what moisture falls from him into the pan: when you have rosted him
sufficiently, you are to hold under him (when you unwind or cut the tape that
ties him) such a dish as you purpose to eat him out of, and let him fall into
it with the sawce that is rosted in his belly; and by this means the Pike *will* 20
be kept unbroken and complete; then to the sawce, which was within him, and
also in the pan, you are to add a fit quantity of the best butter, and to squeeze
the juice of three or four Oranges: lastly, you may either put into the Pike *with*
the Oysters, *two cloves of Garlick, and take it whole out when the* Pike *is*
cut off the spit, or to give the sawce a hogoe, let the dish (into which you let 25
the Pike *fall) be rubed with it; the using or not using of this Garlick is left*
to your discretion.

This dish of meat is too good for any but Anglers or honest men;
and, I trust, you wil prove both, and therefore I have trusted you
with this Secret. And now I shall proceed to give you some Observa- 30
tions concerning the *Carp.*

CHAP. VIII.

Pisc. The *Carp* is a stately, a good, and a subtle fish, a fish that hath not (as it is said) been long in *England*, but said to be by one Mr *Mascall* (a Gentleman then living at *Plumsted* in *Sussex*) brought
5 into this Nation: and for the better confirmation of this, you are to remember I told you that *Gesner* sayes, there is not a *Pike* in *Spain*, and that except the Eele, which lives longest out of the water, there is none that will endure more hardness, or live longer then a *Carp* will out of it, and so the report of his being brought out of a forrain
10 Nation into this, is the more probable.

Carps and *Loches* are observed to breed several months in one year, which most other fish do not, and it is the rather believed, because you shall scarce or never take a *Male Carp* without a *Melt*, or a *Female* without a *Roe* or *Spawn*; and for the most part very much,
15 and especially all the Summer season; and it is observed, that they breed more naturally in Ponds then in running waters, and that those that live in rivers are taken by men of the best palates to be much the better meat.

And it is observed, that in some Ponds *Carps* will not breed,
20 especially in cold Ponds; but where they will breed, they breed innumerably, if there be no *Pikes* nor *Pearch* to devour their Spawn, when it is cast upon grass, or flags, or weeds, where it lies ten or twelve dayes before it be enlivened.

The *Carp*, if he have water room and good feed, will grow to
25 a very great bigness and length: I have heard, to above a yard long; though I never saw one above thirty three inches, which was a very great and goodly fish.

Now as the increase of *Carps* is wonderful for their number: so there is not a reason found out, I think, by any, why they should
30 breed in some Ponds, and not in others of the same nature, for soil and all other circumstances; and as their breeding, so are their decayes also very mysterious; I have both read it, and been told by a Gentleman of tryed honestie, that he has knowne sixtie or

more large *Carps* put into several Ponds neer to a house, where by reason of the stakes in the Ponds, and the Owners constant being neer to them, it was impossible they should be stole away from him, and that when he has after three or four years emptied the Pond, and expected an increase from them by breeding young ones (for 5 that they might do so, he had, as the rule is, put in three Melters for one Spawner) he has, I say, after three or four years found neither a young nor old *Carp* remaining: And the like I have known of one that has almost watched his Pond, and at a like distance of time at the fishing of a Pond, found of seventy or eighty large *Carps* 10 not above five or six: and that he had forborn longer to fish the said Pond, but that he saw in a hot day in Summer, a large *Carp* swim neer to the top of the water with a *Frog* upon his head, and that he upon that occasion caused his Pond to be let dry: and I say, of seventie or eighty *Carps*, only found five or six in the said 15 Pond, and those very sick and lean, and with every one a Frog sticking so fast on the head of the said *Carps*, that the Frog would not bee got off without extreme force or killing, and the Gentleman that did affirm this to me, told me he saw it, and did declare his belief to be (and I also believe the same) that he thought the other 20 *Carps* that were so strangely lost, were so killed by *Frogs*, and then devoured.

But I am faln into this discourse by accident, of which I might say more, but it has proved longer then I intended, and possibly may not to you be considerable; I shall therefore give you three 25 or four more short observations of the *Carp*, and then fall upon some directions how you shall fish for him.

The age of *Carps* is by S. *Francis Bacon* (in his History of Life and Death) observed to be but ten years; yet others think they live longer; but most conclude, that (contrary to the *Pike* or *Luce*) all 30 *Carps* are the better for age and bigness; the tongues of *Carps* are noted to be choice and costly meat, especially to them that buy them; but *Gesner* sayes, *Carps* have no tongues like other fish, but a piece of flesh-like-fish in their mouth like to a tongue, and may be so called, but it is certain it is choicely good, and that the *Carp* 35 is to be reckoned amongst those leather mouthed fish, which I told you have their teeth in their throat, and for that reason he is very seldome lost by breaking his hold, if your hook bee once stuck into his chaps.

I told you, that Sir *Francis Bacon* thinks that the *Carp* lives but ten years; but *Janus Dubravius* (a *Germane* as I think) has writ a book
5 in Latine of Fish and Fish Ponds, in which he says, that *Carps* begin to Spawn at the age of three years, and continue to do so till thirty; he sayes also, that in the time of their breeding, which is in Summer when the Sun hath warmed both the earth and water, and so apted them also for generation, that then three or four Male *Carps* will
10 follow a Female, and that then she putting on a seeming coyness, they force her through weeds and flags, where she lets fall her eggs or Spawn, which sticks fast to the weeds, and then they let fall their Melt upon it, and so it becomes in a short time to be a living fish; and, as I told you, it is thought the *Carp* does this several months
15 in the yeer, and most believe that most fish breed after this manner, except the Eele: and it is thought that all *Carps* are not bred by generation, but that some breed otherwayes, as some *Pikes* do.

Much more might be said out of him, and out of *Aristotle*, which *Dubravius* often quotes in his Discourse, but it might rather perplex
20 then satisfie you, and therefore I shall rather chuse to direct you how to catch, then spend more time in discoursing either of the nature or the breeding of this *Carp*, or of any more circumstances

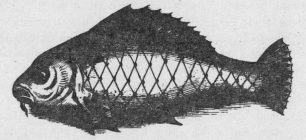

concerning him, but yet I shall remember you of what I told you before, that he is a very subtle fish and hard to be caught.
25 And my first direction is, that if you will fish for a *Carp*, you must put on a very large measure of *patience*, especially to fish for a *River Carp*: I have knowne a very good Fisher angle diligently four or six hours in a day, for three or four dayes together for a

River Carp, and not have a bite: and you are to note, that in some Ponds it is as hard to catch a *Carp* as in a River; that is to say, where they have store of feed, and the water is of a clayish colour; but you are to remember, that I have told you there is no rule without an exception, and therefore being possest with that hope 5 and patience which I wish to all fishers, especially to the *Carp-Angler*, I shall tell you with what bait to fish for him; but that must be either early or late, and let me tell you, that in hot weather (for he will seldome bite in cold) you cannot bee too early or too late at it. 10

The *Carp* bites either at wormes or at Paste; and of worms I think the blewish Marsh or Meadow worm is best; but possibly another worm not too big may do as well, and so may a Gentle; and as for Pastes, there are almost as many sorts as there are Medicines for the Toothach, but doubtless sweet Pastes are best; I mean, Pastes 15 mixt with honey, or with Sugar; which, that you may the better beguile this crafty fish, should be thrown into the Pond or place in which you fish for him some hours before you undertake your tryal of skil by the Angle-Rod: and doubtless, if it be thrown into the water a day or two before, at several times, and in smal pellets, 20 you are the likelier when you fish for the *Carp*, to obtain your desired sport: or in a large Pond, to draw them to any certain place, that they may the better and with more hope be fished for; You are to throw into it, in some certaine place, either grains, or bloud mixt with Cow-dung, or with bran; or any Garbage, as Chickens guts 25 or the like, and then some of your smal sweet pellets, with which you purpose to angle; these smal pellets, being few of them thrown in as you are Angling.

And your Paste must bee thus made: Take the flesh of a Rabet or Cat cut smal, and Bean-flower, or (if not easily got then) other 30 flowre, and then mix these together, and put to them either sugar, or Honey, which I think better, and then beat these together in a Mortar; or sometimes work them in your hands, (your hands being very clean) and then make it into a ball, or two, or three, as you like best for your use: but you must work or pound it so long in 35 the Mortar, as to make it so tough as to hang upon your hook without washing from it, yet not too hard; or that you may the better keep it on your hook, you may kneade with your Paste a little (and not much) white or yellowish wool.

And if you would have this Paste keep all the year for any other fish, then mix with it *Virgins-wax* and *clarified honey*, and work them
5 together with your hands before the fire; then make these into balls, and it will keep all the yeer.

And if you fish for a *Carp* with Gentles, then put upon your hook a small piece of Scarlet about this bigness ■, it being soked in, or annointed with *Oyl of Peter*, called by some, *Oyl of the Rock*; and
10 if your Gentles be put two or three dayes before into a box of horn anointed with Honey, and so put upon your hook, as to preserve them to be living, you are as like to kill this craftie fish this way as any other; but still as you are fishing, chaw a little white or brown bread in your mouth, and cast it into the Pond about
15 the place where your flote swims. Other baits there be, but these with diligence, and patient watchfulness, will do it as well as any as I have ever practised, or heard of: and yet I shall tell you, that the crumbs of white bread and honey made into a Paste, is a good bait for a *Carp*, and you know it is more easily made. And having
20 said thus much of the *Carp*, my next discourse shal be of the *Bream*, which shall not prove so tedious, and therefore I desire the continuance of your attention.

CHAP. IX.

Pisc. The *Bream* being at a full growth, is a large and stately fish; he will breed both in Rivers and Ponds, but loves best to live in Ponds, where, if he likes the aire, he will grow not only to be very large, but as fat as a Hog: he is by *Gesner* taken to be more pleasant or sweet then wholesome; this fish is long in growing, but breeds exceedingly in a water that pleases him, yea, in many Ponds so fast, as to over store them, and starve the other fish.

The Baits good for to catch the *Bream* are many; as namely, young Wasps, and a Paste made of brown bread and honey, or Gentels, or especially a worm, a worm that is not much unlike a Magot, which you will find at the roots of *Docks*, or of *Flags*, or of *Rushes* that grow in the water, or watry places, and a *Grashopper* having his legs nip'd off, or a flye that is in *June* and *July* to be found amongst the green Reed, growing by the water side, those are said to bee excellent baits. I doubt not but there be many others that both the *Bream* and the *Carp* also would bite at; but these time and experience will teach you how to find out: And so having according to my promise given you these short Observations concerning the *Bream*, I shall also give you some Observations concerning the *Tench*, and those also very briefly.

The *Tench* is observed to love to live in Ponds; but if he be in a River, then in the still places of the River; he is observed to be a Physician to other fishes, and is so called by many that have been searchers into the nature of fish; and it is said, that a *Pike* will neither devour nor hurt him, because the *Pike* being sick or hurt by any accident, is cured by touching the *Tench*, and the *Tench* does the like to other fishes, either by touching them, or by being in their company.

Randelitius sayes in his discourse of fishes (quoted by *Gesner*) that at his being at *Rome*, he saw certaine Jewes apply *Tenches* to the feet of a sick man for a cure; and it is observed, that many of those people have many Secrets unknown to Christians, secrets which

have never been written, but have been successively since the dayes
of *Solomon* (who knew the nature of all things from the Shrub to
the Cedar) delivered by tradition from the father to the son, and
so from generation to generation without writing, or (unless it were
5 casually) without the least communicating them to any other
Nation or Tribe (for to do so, they account a profanation): yet this
fish, that does by a natural inbred Balsome, not only cure himselfe
if he be wounded, but others also, loves not to live in clear streams
paved with gravel, but in standing waters, where mud and the
10 worst of weeds abound, and therefore it is, I think, that this *Tench*

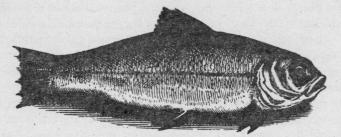

is by so many accounted better for Medicines then for meat: but for
the first, I am able to say little; and for the later, can say positively,
that he eats pleasantly; and will therefore give you a few, and but
a few directions how to catch him.

5   He will bite at a Paste made of brown bread and honey, or at
a Marsh-worm, or a Lob-worm; he will bite also at a smaller worm,
with his head nip'd off, and a cod-worm put on the hook before
the worm; and I doubt not but that he will also in the three hot
months (for in the nine colder he stirs not much) bite at a Flag-
20 worm, or at a green Gentle, but can positively say no more of the
Tench, he being a fish that I have not often Angled for; but I wish
my honest Scholer may, and be ever fortunate when hee fishes.

    Viat. I thank you good Master: but I pray Sir, since you see it
still rains *May* butter, give me some observations and directions
25 concerning the *Pearch*, for they say he is both a very good and a
bold biting fish, and I would fain learne to fish for him.

    Pisc. You say true, Scholer, the *Pearch* is a very good, and a very
bold biting fish: he is one of the fishes of prey, that, like the *Pike*

and *Trout*, carries his teeth in his mouth, not in his throat, and dare venture to kill and devour another fish; this fish, and the *Pike* are (sayes *Gesner*) the best of fresh water fish; he Spawns but once a year, and is by Physicians held very nutritive; yet by many to be hard of digestion: They abound more in the River *Poe*, and in England, (sayes *Randelitius*) then other parts, and have in their brain a stone, which is in forrain parts sold by Apothecaries, being there noted to be very medicinable against the stone in the reins: These be a part of the commendations which some Philosophycal brains have bestowed upon the fresh-water *Pearch*, yet they commend the Sea *Pearch*, which is known by having but one fin on his back, (of which they say, we *English* see but a few) to be a much better fish.

The *Pearch* grows slowly, yet will grow, as I have been credibly informed, to be almost two foot long; for my Informer told me, such a one was not long taken by Sir *Abraham Williams*, a Gentleman of worth, and a lover of Angling, that yet lives, and I wish he may: this was a deep bodied fish; and doubtless durst have devoured a *Pike* of half his own length; for I have told you, he is a bold fish, such a one, as but for extreme hunger, the *Pike* will not devour; for to affright the *Pike*, the *Pearch* will set up his fins, much like as a *Turkie-Cock* wil sometimes set up his tail.

But, my Scholer, the *Pearch* is not only valiant to defend himself, but he is (as you said) a bold biting fish, yet he will not bite at all seasons of the yeer; he is very abstemious in Winter; and hath been observed by some, not usually to bite till the *Mulberry tree* buds, that is to say, till extreme Frosts be past for that Spring; for when the *Mulberry tree* blossomes, many Gardners observe their forward fruit to be past the danger of Frosts, and some have made the like observation of the *Pearches* biting.

But bite the *Pearch* will, and that very boldly; and as one has wittily observed, if there be twentie or fortie in a hole, they may be at one standing all catch'd one after another; they being, as he saies, like the wicked of the world, not afraid, though their fellowes and companions perish in their sight.

And the baits for this bold fish are not many; I mean, he will bite as well at some, or at any of these three, as at any or all others whatsoever; a *Worm*, a *Minnow*, or a little *Frog* (of which you may

find many in hay time); and of *worms*, the Dunghill worm, called a *brandling*, I take to be best, being well scowred in Moss or Fennel; and if you fish for a *Pearch* with a *Minnow*, then it is best to be alive, you sticking your hook through his back fin, and letting him
5 swim up and down about mid-water, or a little lower, and you still keeping him to about that depth, by a Cork, which ought not to be a very light one: and the like way you are to fish for the *Pearch* with a small *Frog*, your hook being fastened through the skin of his leg, towards the upper part of it: And lastly, I will give you
10 but this advise, that you give the *Pearch* time enough when he bites, for there was scarse ever any *Angler* that has given him too much. And now I think best to rest my selfe, for I have almost spent my spirits with talking so long.

Viat. Nay, good Master, one fish more, for you see it rains still,
15 and you know our Angles are like money put to usury; they may thrive though we sit still and do nothing, but talk and enjoy one another. Come, come the other fish, good Master.

Pisc. But Scholer, have you nothing to mix with this Discourse, which now grows both tedious and tiresome? shall I have nothing
20 from you that seems to have both a good memorie, and a chearful Spirit?

Viat. Yes, Master, I will speak you a Coppie of Verses that were made by Doctor *Donne*, and made to shew the world that hee could make soft and smooth Verses, when he thought them fit and worth
25 his labour; and I love them the better, because they allude to Rivers, and fish, and fishing. They bee these:

Come live with me, and be my love,
And we will some new pleasures prove,
Of golden sands, and Christal brooks,
With silken lines and silver hooks.

There will the River wispering run,   5
Warm'd by thy eyes more then the Sun;
And there th'inamel'd fish wil stay,
Begging themselves they may betray.

When thou wilt swim in that live bath,
Each fish, which every channel hath   10
Most amorously to thee will swim,
Gladder to catch thee, then thou him.

If thou, to be so seen, beest loath
By Sun or Moon, thou darknest both;
And, if mine eyes have leave to see,   15
I need not their light, having thee.

Let others freeze with Angling Reeds,
And cut their legs with shels and weeds,
Or treacherously poor fish beset,
With strangling snares, or windowy net.   20

Let coarse bold hands, from slimy nest,
The bedded fish in banks outwrest,
Let curious Traitors sleave silk flies,
To 'witch poor wandring fishes eyes.

For thee, thou needst no such deceit,   25
For thou thy self art thine own bait;
That fish that is not catch'd thereby,
Is wiser far, alas, then I.

Pisc. Well remembered, honest Scholer, I thank you for these
choice Verses, which I have heard formerly, but had quite forgot, 30
till they were recovered by your happie memorie. Well, being I
have now, rested my self a little, I will make you some requital,
by telling you some observations of the *Eele*, for it rains still, and
(as you say) our Angles are as money put to Use, that thrive when
we play.   35

It is agreed by most men, that the *Eele* is both a good and a most
daintie fish; but most men differ about his breeding; some say,
they breed by generation as other fish do; and others, that they
5 breed (as some worms do) out of the putrifaction of the earth, and
divers other waies; those that denie them to breed by generation,
as other fish do, ask, if any man ever saw an *Eel* to have Spawn
or Melt? and they are answered, That they may be as certain of
their breeding, as if they had seen Spawn; for they say, that they
10 are certain that *Eeles* have all parts fit for generation, like other
fish, but so smal as not to be easily discerned, by reason of their
fatness; but that discerned they may be; and that the Hee and the
She *Eele* may be distinguished by their fins.

And others say, that *Eeles* growing old, breed other *Eeles* out of
15 the corruption of their own age, which Sir *Francis Bacon* sayes,
exceeds not ten years. And others say, that *Eeles* are bred off a particular dew falling in the Months of *May* or *June* on the banks of
some particular Ponds or Rivers (apted by nature for that end)
which in a few dayes is by the Suns heat turned into *Eeles*. I have
20 seen in the beginning of *July*, in a River not far from *Canterbury*,
some parts of it covered over with young *Eeles* about the thickness
of a straw; and these *Eeles* did lye on the top of that water, as thick
as motes are said to be in the Sun; and I have heard the like of
other Rivers, as namely, in *Severn*, and in a *pond* or *Mere* in *Stafford-*
25 *shire*, where about a set time in Summer, such small *Eeles* abound
so much, that many of the poorer sort of people, that inhabit near
to it, take such *Eeles* out of this Mere, with sieves or sheets, and
make a kind of *Eele-cake* of them, and eat it like as bread. And *Gesner*
quotes venerable *Bede* to say, that in *England* there is an Iland called
30 *Ely*, by reason of the innumerable number of *Eeles* that breed in
it. But that *Eeles* may be bred as some worms and some kind of
Bees and *Wasps* are, either of dew, or out of the corruption of the
earth, seems to be made probable by the *Barnacles* and young

Goslings bred by the suns heat and the rotten planks of an old Ship, and hatched of trees, both which are related for truths by *Dubartas*, and our learned *Cambden*, and laborious *Gerrard* in his *Herball*.

It is said by *Randelitius*, that those *Eeles* that are bred in Rivers, that relate to, or be neer to the Sea, never return to the fresh waters (as the *Salmon* does alwaies desire to do) when they have once tasted the salt water; and I do the more easily believe this, because I am certain that powdered Bief is a most excellent bait to catch an *Eele*: and Sir *Francis Bacon* will allow the *Eeles* life to be but ten years; yet he in his History of Life and Death, mentions a *Lamprey*, belonging to the *Roman* Emperor, to be made tame, and so kept for almost threescore yeers; and that such useful and pleasant observations were made of this *Lamprey*, that *Crassus* the Oratour (who kept her) lamented her death.

It is granted by all, or most men, that *Eeles*, for about six months (that is to say, the six cold months of the yeer) stir not up and down, neither in the Rivers nor the Pools in which they are, but get into the soft earth or mud, and there many of them together bed themselves, and live without feeding upon any thing (as I have told you some *Swallows* have been observed to do in hollow trees for those six cold months); and this the *Eele* and *Swallow* do, as not being able to endure winter weather; for *Gesner* quotes *Albertus* to say, that in the yeer 1125 (that years winter being more cold then usual) *Eeles* did by natures instinct get out of the water into a stack of hay in a Meadow upon dry ground, and there bedded themselves, but yet at last died there. I shall say no more of the *Eele*, but that, as it is observed, he is impatient of cold, so it has been observed, that in warm weather an *Eele* has been known to live five days out of the water. And lastly, let me tell you, that some curious searchers into the natures of fish, observe that there be several sorts or kinds of *Eeles*, as the *silver-Eele*, and the green or *greenish Eel* (with which the River of Thames abounds, and are called *Gregs*); and a blackish *Eele*, whose head is more flat and bigger then ordinary *Eeles*; and also an *Eele* whose fins are redish, and but seldome taken in this Nation (and yet taken sometimes): These several kinds of *Eeles*, are (say some) diversly bred; as namely, out of the corruption of the earth, and by dew, and other wayes (as

I have said to you:) and yet it is affirmed by some, that for a certain, the *Silver-Eele* breeds by generation, but not by Spawning as other fish do, but that her Brood come alive from her no bigger nor longer then a pin, and I have had too many testimonies of this to doubt
5 the truth of it.

And this *Eele* of which I have said so much to you, may be caught with divers kinds of baits; as namely, with powdered Bief, with a *Lob* or *Garden-worm*, with a *Minnow*, or gut of a *Hen*, *Chicken*, or with almost any thing, for he is a greedy fish: but the *Eele* seldome stirs in
10 the day, but then hides himselfe, and therefore he is usually caught by night, with one of these baits of which I have spoken, and then caught by laying hooks, which you are to fasten to the bank, or twigs of a tree; or by throwing a string cross the stream, with many hooks at it, and baited with the foresaid baits, and a clod or
15 plummet, or stone, thrown into the River with this line, that so you may in the morning find it neer to some fixt place, and then take it up with a drag-hook or otherwise: but these things are indeed too common to be spoken of; and an hours fishing with any *Angler* will teach you better, both for these, and many other common things
20 in the practical part of *Angling*, then a weeks discourse. I shall therefore conclude this direction for taking the *Eele*, by telling you, that in a warm day in Summer, I have taken many a good *Eele* by *snigling*, and have been much pleased with that sport.

And because you that are but a young Angler, know not what
25 *snigling* is, I wil now teach it to you: you remember I told you that *Eeles* do not usually stir in the day time, for then they hide themselves under some covert, or under boards, or planks about Floud-gates, or Weirs, or Mils, or in holes in the River banks; and you observing your time in a warm day, when the water is lowest, may take a
30 hook tied to a strong line, or to a string about a yard long, and then into one of these holes, or between any boards about a Mill, or under any great stone or plank, or any place where you think an *Eele* may hide or shelter her selfe, there with the help of a short stick put in your bait, but leisurely, and as far as you may con-
35 veniently; and it is scarce to be doubted, but that if there be an *Eel* within the sight of it, the *Eele* will bite instantly, and as certainly gorge it; and you need not doubt to have him, if you pull him not

out of the hole too quickly, but pull him out by degrees, for he lying folded double in his hole, will, with the help of his taile, break all, unless you give him time to be wearied with pulling, and so get him out by degrees; not pulling too hard. And thus much for this present time concerning the *Eele*: I will next tel you a little 5 of the *Barbell*, and hope with a little discourse of him, to have an end of this showr, and fal to fishing, for the weather clears up a little.

CHAP. XI.

Pisc. The *Barbell*, is so called (sayes *Gesner*) from or by reason of his beard, or wattels at his mouth, his mouth being under his nose or chaps, and he is one of the leather mouthed fish that has
5 his teeth in his throat; he loves to live in very swift streams, and where it is gravelly, and in the gravel will root or dig with his nose like a Hog, and there nest himself, taking so fast hold of any weeds or moss that grows on stones, or on piles about *Weirs*, or *Floud-gates*, or *Bridges*, that the water is not able, be it never so swift, to force
10 him from the place which he seems to contend for: this is his constant custome in Summer, when both he, and most living creatures joy and sport themselves in the Sun; but at the approach of Winter, then he forsakes the swift streams and shallow waters, and by degrees retires to those parts of the River that are quiet and deeper; in which
15 places, (and I think about that time) he Spawns; and as I have formerly told you, with the help of the Melter, hides his Spawn or eggs in holes, which they both dig in the gravel, and then they mutually labour to cover it with the same sand to prevent it from being devoured by other fish.

20 There be such store of this fish in the River *Danubie*, that *Randelitius* sayes, they may in some places of it, and in some months of the yeer, be taken by those that dwell neer to the River, with their hands, eight or ten load at a time; he sayes, they begin to be good in *May*, and that they cease to be so in *August*; but it is
25 found to be otherwise in this Nation: but thus far we agree with him, that the Spawne of a *Barbell* is, if it be not poison, as he sayes, yet that it is dangerous meat, and especially in the month of *May*; and *Gesner* declares, it had an ill effect upon him, to the indangering of his life.

30 This fish is of a fine case and handsome shape, and may be rather said not be ill, then to bee good meat; the *Chub* and he have (I think) both lost a part of their credit by ill Cookery, they being reputed the worst or coarsest of fresh water fish: but the *Barbell* affords

an *Angler* choice sport, being a lustie and a cunning fish; so lustie
and cunning as to endanger the breaking of the Anglers line, by
running his head forcibly towards any covert or hole, or bank, and
then striking at the line, to break it off with his tail (as is observed
by *Plutark*, in his book *De industria animalium*) and also so cunning 5
to nibble and suck off your worme close to the hook, and yet avoid
the letting the hook come into his mouth.

The *Barbell* is also curious for his baits, that is to say, that they
be clean and sweet; that is to say, to have your worms well scowred,
and not kept in sowre or mustie moss; for at a well scowred Lob- 10
worm, he will bite as boldly as at any bait, especially, if the night
or two before you fish for him, you shall bait the places where you
intend to fish for him with big worms cut into pieces: and Gentles
(not being too much scowred, but green) are a choice bait for him,
and so is cheese, which is not to be too hard, but kept a day or 15
two in a wet linnen cloth to make it tough; with this you may also
bait the water a day or two before you fish for the *Barbel*, and be
much the likelier to catch store; and if the cheese were laid in
clarified honey a short time before (as namely, an hour or two)
you were still the likelier to catch fish; some have directed to cut 20
the cheese into thin pieces, and toste it, and then tye it on the hook
with fine Silk: and some advise to fish for the *Barbell* with Sheeps
tallow and soft cheese beaten or work'd into a Paste, and that it
is choicely good in *August*; and I believe it: but doubtless the Lob-
worm well scoured, and the Gentle not too much scowred, and 25
cheese ordered as I have directed, are baits enough, and I think
will serve in any Month; though I shall commend any Angler that
tryes conclusions, and is industrious to improve the Art. And now,

my honest Scholer, the long showre, and my tedious discourse are both ended together; and I shall give you but this Observation, That when you fish for a *Barbell*, your Rod and Line be both long, and of good strength, for you will find him a heavy and a doged
5 fish to be dealt withal, yet he seldom or never breaks his hold if he be once strucken.

And now lets go and see what interest the *Trouts* will pay us for letting our *Angle-rods* lye so long and so quietly in the water. Come, Scholer; which will you take up?

10 *Viat*. Which you think fit, Master.

Pisc. Why, you shall take up that; for I am certain by viewing the Line, it has a fish at it. Look you, Scholer, well done. Come now, take up the other too; well, now you may tell my brother *Peter* at night, that you have caught a lease of *Trouts* this day. And
15 now lets move toward our lodging, and drink a draught of *Red*-Cows milk, as we go, and give pretty *Maudlin* and her mother a brace of *Trouts* for their supper.

Viat. Master, I like your motion very well, and I think it is now about milking time, and yonder they be at it.

20 *Pisc*. God speed you good woman, I thank you both for our Songs last night; I and my companion had such fortune a fishing this day, that we resolve to give you and *Maudlin* a brace of *Trouts* for supper, and we will now taste a draught of your *Red Cows milk*.

Milkw. Marry, and that you shal with all my heart, and I will
25 be still your debtor: when you come next this way, if you will but speak the word, I will make you a good *Sillabub*, and then you may sit down in a *Hay-cock* and eat it, and *Maudlin* shal sit by and sing you the good old Song of the *Hunting in Chevy Chase*, or some other good Ballad, for she hath good store of them: *Maudlin* hath
30 a notable memory.

Viat. We thank you, and intend once in a Month to call upon you again, and give you a little warning, and so good night; good night *Maudlin*. And now, good Master, lets lose no time, but tell me somewhat more of fishing; and if you please, first something
35 of fishing for a *Gudgion*.

Pisc. I will, honest Scholer. The *Gudgion* is an excellent fish to eat, and good also to enter a young *Angler*; he is easie to bee taken with a smal red worm at the ground and is one of those leather mouthed fish that has his teeth in his throat, and will hardly be lost off from the hook if he be once strucken: they be usually scattered up and down every River in the shallows, in the heat of Summer; but in *Autome*, when the weeds begin to grow sowre 5 or rot, and the weather colder, then they gather together, and get into the deeper parts of the water, and are to be fish'd for there, with your hook alwaies touching the ground, if you fish for him with a flote or with a cork; but many will fish for the *Gudgion* by hand, with a running line upon the ground without a cork as a 10 *Trout* is fished for, and it is an excellent way.

There is also another fish called a *Pope*, and by some a *Ruffe*, a fish that is not known to be in some Rivers; it is much like the *Pearch* for his shape, but will not grow to be bigger then a *Gudgion*; he is an excellent fish, no fish that swims is of a pleasanter 15 taste; and he is also excellent to enter a young *Angler*, for he is a greedy biter, and they will usually lye abundance of them together in one reserved place where the water is deep, and runs quietly; and an easie Angler, if he has found where they lye, may catch fortie or fiftie, or sometimes twice so many at a standing. 20

There is also a *Bleak*, a fish that is ever in motion, and therefore called by some the River Swallow; for just as you shall observe the *Swallow* to be most evenings in Summer ever in motion, making short and quick turns when he flies to catch flies in the aire, by which he lives, so does the *Bleak* at the top of the water; and this 25 fish is best caught with a fine smal Artificial Fly, which is to be of a brown colour, and very smal, and the hook answerable: There is no better sport then whiping for *Bleaks* in a boat in a Summers evening, with a hazle top about five or six foot long, and a line twice the length of the Rod. I have heard Sir *Henry Wotton* say, 30 that there be many that in *Italy* will catch *Swallows* so, or especially *Martins* (the Bird-Angler standing on the top of a Steeple to do it, and with a line twice so long, as I have spoke of) and let me tell you, Scholer, that both *Martins* and *Blekes* be most excellent meat. 35

I might now tell you how to catch *Roch* and *Dace*, and some other fish of little note, that I have not yet spoke of; but you see we are

almost at our lodging, and indeed if we were not, I would omit
to give you any directions concerning them, or how to fish for them,
not but that they be both good fish (being in season) and especially
to some palates, and they also make the Angler good sport (and
5 you know the Hunter sayes, there is more sport in hunting the Hare,
then in eating of her) but I will forbear to give you any direction
concerning them, because you may go a few dayes and take the
pleasure of the fresh aire, and bear any common Angler company
that fishes for them, and by that means learn more then any direc-
10 tion I can give you in words, can make you capable of; and I will
therefore end my discourse, for yonder comes our brother *Peter* and
honest *Coridon*, but I will promise you that as you and I fish, and
walk to morrow towards *London*, if I have now forgotten any thing,
that I can then remember, I will not keep it from you.

15 Well met, Gentlemen, this is luckie that we meet so just together
at this very door. Come Hostis, where are you? is Supper ready?
come, first give us drink, and be as quick as you can, for I believe
wee are all very hungry. Wel, brother *Peter* and *Coridon* to you both;
come drink and tell me what luck of fish: we two have caught but
20 ten *Trouts*, of which my Scholer caught three; look here's eight,
and a brace we gave away: we have had a most pleasant day for
fishing, and talking, and now returned home both weary and
hungry, and now meat and rest will be pleasant.

Pet. And *Coridon* and I have not had an unpleasant day, and yet
25 I have caught but five *Trouts*; for indeed we went to a good honest
Ale-house, and there we plaid at shovel-board half the day; all the
time that it rained we were there, and as merry as they that fish'd,
and I am glad we are now with a dry house over our heads, for
heark how it rains and blows. Come Hostis, give us more Ale, and
30 our Supper with what haste you may, and when we have sup'd,
lets have your Song, *Piscator*, and the Ketch that your Scholer
promised us, or else *Coridon* wil be doged.

Pisc. Nay, I will not be worse then my word, you shall not want
my Song, and I hope I shall be perfect in it.

35 *Viat.* And I hope the like for my Ketch, which I have ready too,
and therefore lets go merrily to Supper, and then have a gentle
touch at singing and drinking; but the last with moderation.

Cor. Come, now for your Song, for we have fed heartily. Come Hostis, give us a little more drink, and lay a few more sticks on the fire, and now sing when you will.

Pisc. Well then, here's to you *Coridon*; and now for my Song.

> *Oh the brave Fishers life,*   5
> *It is the best of any,*
> *'Tis full of pleasure, void of strife,*
> *And 'tis belov'd of many:*
> > *Other joyes*
> > *are but toyes,*   10
> > *only this*
> > *lawful is,*
> > *for our skil*
> > *breeds no ill,*
> *but content and pleasure.*   15
>
> *In a morning up we rise*
> *Ere* Aurora's *peeping,*
> *Drink a cup to wash our eyes,*
> *Leave the sluggard sleeping;*
> > *Then we go*   20
> > *too and fro,*
> > *with our knacks*
> > *at our backs,*
> > *to such streams*
> > *as the* Thames   25
> *if we have the leisure.*
>
> *When we please to walk abroad*
> *For our recreation,*
> *In the fields is our abode,*
> *Full of delectation:*   30
> > *Where in a Brook*
> > *with a hook,*
> > *or a Lake*
> > *fish we take,*
> > *there we sit*   35
> > *for a bit,*
> *till we fish intangle.*

We have Gentles in a horn,
We have Paste and worms too,
We can watch both night and morn,
Suffer rain and storms too:
5   *None do here*
      use to swear,
      oathes do fray
      fish away,
      we sit still,
10   *watch our quill,*
Fishers must not rangle.

If the Suns excessive heat
Make our bodies swelter,
To an Osier *hedge we get*
15 *For a friendly shelter,*
      where in a dike
      Pearch *or* Pike,
      Roch *or* Dace
      we do chase
20   Bleak *or* Gudgion
      without grudging,
we are still contented.

Or we sometimes pass an hour,
Under a green willow,
25 *That defends us from a showr,*
Making earth our pillow,
      There we may
      think and pray
      before death
30   *stops our breath;*
      other joyes
      are but toyes
and to be lamented.

Viat. Well sung, Master; this dayes fortune and pleasure, and
35 this nights company and Song, do all make me more and more
in love with *Angling.* Gentlemen, my Master left me alone for an
hour this day, and I verily believe he retir'd himself from talking

with me, that he might be so perfect in this Song; was it not Master?

Pisc. Yes indeed, for it is many yeers since I learn'd it, and having forgotten a part of it, I was forced to patch it up by the help of my own invention, who am not excellent at Poetry, as my part of the Song may testifie: But of that I will say no more, least you should think I meant by discommending it, to beg your commendations of it. And therefore without replications, lets hear your Ketch, Scholer, which I hope will be a good one, for you are both Musical, and have a good fancie to boot.

Viat. Marry, and that you shall, and as freely as I would have my honest Master tel me some more secrets of fish and fishing as we walk and fish towards *London* to morrow. But Master, first let me tell you, that that very hour which you were absent from me, I sate down under a Willow tree by the water side, and considered what you had told me of the owner of that pleasant Meadow in which you then left me, that he had a plentiful estate, and not a heart to think so; that he had at this time many Law Suites depending, and that they both damp'd his mirth and took up so much of his time and thoughts, that he himselfe had not leisure to take the sweet content that I, who pretended no title, took in his fields; for I could there sit quietly, and looking on the water, see fishes leaping at Flies of several shapes and colours; looking on the Hils, could behold them spotted with Woods and Groves; looking down the Meadows, could see here a Boy gathering *Lillies* and *Lady-smocks*, and there a Girle cropping *Culverkeys* and *Cowslips*, all to make Garlands sutable to this pleasant Month of *May*; these and many other Field-Flowers so perfum'd the air, that I thought this Meadow like the field in *Sicily* (of which *Diodorus* speaks) where the perfumes arising from the place, makes all dogs that hunt in it, to fall and to lose their hottest sent. I say, as I thus sate joying in mine own happy condition, and pittying that rich mans that ought this, and many other pleasant Groves and Meadows about me, I did thankfully remember what my Saviour said, that *the meek possess the earth*; for indeed they are free from those high, those restless thoughts and contentions which corrode the sweets of life. For they, and they only, can say as the Poet has happily exprest it,

> *Hail blest estate of poverty!*
> *Happy enjoyment of such minds,*
> *As rich in low contentedness,*
> *Can, like the reeds in roughest winds,*
> 5   *By yeelding make that blow but smal*
>   *At which proud Oaks and Cedars fal.*

Gentlemen, these were a part of the thoughts that then possest me, and I there made a conversion of a piece of an old Ketch, and added more of it, fitting them to be sung by us Anglers: Come, 10 Master, you can sing well, you must sing a part of it as it is in this paper.[1]

> *Man's life is but vain;*
> *For 'tis subject to pain,*
> *And sorrow, and short as a bubble;*
> 15 *'Tis a hodge podge of business*
> *And money, and care,*
> *And care, and money and trouble.*
> *But we'll take no care*
> *When the weather proves fair*
> 20 *Nor will we vex now, though it rain;*
> *We'll banish all sorrow*
> *And sing till to morrow,*
> *And Angle and Angle again.*

Pet. I marry Sir, this is Musick indeed, this has cheered my heart, 25 and made me to remember six Verses in praise of Musick, which I will speak to you instantly.

> *Musick, miraculous Rhetorick, that speak'st sense*
> *Without a tongue, excelling eloquence;*
> *With what ease might thy errors be excus'd*
> 30 *Wert thou as truly lov'd as th'art abus'd.*
> *But though dull souls neglect, and some reprove thee,*
> *I cannot hate thee, 'cause the Angels love thee.*

Pisc. Well remembered, brother *Peter*, these Verses came seasonably. Come, we will all joine together, mine Hoste and all, and

---

[1] Editor's note: see Appendix, pp. 126‑7, and Notes, p. 148.

sing my Scholers Ketch over again, and then each man drink the tother cup and to bed, and thank God we have a dry house over our heads.

Pisc. Well now, good night to every body.

Pet. And so say I.   5

Viat. And so say I.

Cor. Good night to you all, and I thank you.

Pisc. Good morrow brother *Peter*, and the like to you, honest *Coridon*; come, my Hostis sayes there is seven shillings to pay, lets each man drink a pot for his mornings draught, and lay downe   10 his two shillings, that so my Hostis may not have occasion to repent her self of being so diligent, and using us so kindly.

Pet. The motion is liked by every body; And so Hostis, here's your mony, we Anglers are all beholding to you, it wil not be long ere Ile see you again. And now brother *Piscator*, I wish you and   15 my brother your Scholer a fair day, and good fortune. Come *Coridon*, this is our way.

CHAP. XII.

Viat. Good Master, as we go now towards *London*, be still so courteous as to give me more instructions, for I have several boxes in
my memory in which I will keep them all very safe, there shall
5 not one of them be lost.

Pisc. Well Scholer, that I will, and I will hide nothing from you
that I can remember, and may help you forward towards a perfection in this Art; and because we have so much time, and I have
said so little of *Roch* and *Dace*, I will give you some directions con-
10 cerning some several kinds of baits with which they be usually taken;
they will bite almost at any flies, but especially at Ant-flies;
concerning which, take this direction, for it is very good.

Take the blackish *Ant-fly* out of the Mole-hill, or Ant-hil, in which
place you shall find them in the Months of *June*; or if that be too
15 early in the yeer, then doubtless you may find them in *July*,
August, and most of *September*; gather them alive with both their
wings, and then put them into a glass, that will hold a quart or
a pottle; but first, put into the glass, a handful or more of the moist
earth out of which you gather them, and as much of the roots of
20 the grass of the said Hillock; and then put in the flies gently, that
they lose not their wings, and so many as are put into the glass
without bruising, will live there a month or more, and be alwaies
in a readiness for you to fish with; but if you would have them
keep longer, then get any great earthen pot or barrel of three or
25 four gallons (which is better) then wash your barrel with water
and honey; and having put into it a quantitie of earth and grass
roots, then put in your flies and cover it, and they will live a quarter
of a year; these in any stream and clear water are a deadly bait
for *Roch* or *Dace*, or for a *Chub*, and your rule is to fish not less
30 then a handful from the bottom.

I shall next tell you a winter bait for a *Roch*, a *Dace*, or *Chub*,
and it is choicely good. About *All-hollantide* (and so till Frost comes)
when you see men ploughing up heath-ground, or sandy ground,

or greenswards, then follow the plough, and you shall find a white worm, as big as two Magots, and it hath a red head, (you may observe in what ground most are, for there the Crows will be very watchful, and follow the Plough very close) it is all soft, and full of whitish guts; a worm that is in *Norfolk*, and some other Countries 5 called a *Grub*, and is bred of the spawn or eggs of a Beetle, which she leaves in holes that she digs in the ground under Cow or Horse-dung, and there rests all Winter, and in *March* or *April* comes to be first a red, and then a black Beetle: gather a thousand or two of these, and put them with a peck or two of their own earth into 10 some tub or firkin, and cover and keep them so warm, that the frost or cold air, or winds kill them not, and you may keep them all winter and kill fish with them at any time, and if you put some of them into a little earth and honey a day before you use them, you will find them an excellent baite for *Breame* or *Carp*. 15

And after this manner you may also keep *Gentles* all winter, which is a good bait then, and much the better for being lively and tuffe, or you may breed and keep Gentles thus: Take a piece of beasts liver and with a cross stick, hang it in some corner over a pot or barrel half full of dry clay, and as the Gentles grow big, they wil 20 fall into the barrel and scowre themselves, and be alwayes ready for use whensoever you incline to fish; and these Gentles may be thus made til after *Michaelmas*: But if you desire to keep Gentles to fish with all the yeer, then get a dead *Cat* or a *Kite*, and let it be fly-blowne, and when the Gentles begin to be alive and to 25 stir, then bury it and them in moist earth, but as free from frost as you can, and these you may dig up at any time when you intend to use them; these wil last till *March*, and about that time turn to be flies.

But if you be nice to fowl your fingers (which good Anglers seldome 30 are) then take this bait: Get a handful of well made Mault, and put it into a dish of water, and then wash and rub it betwixt your hands til you make it cleane, and as free from husks as you can; then put that water from it, and put a smal quantitie of fresh water to it, and set it in something that is fit for that purpose, over the 35 fire, where it is not to boil apace, but leisurely, and very softly, until it become somewhat soft, which you may try by feeling it

betwixt your finger and thumb; and when it is soft, then put your water from it, and then take a sharp knife, and turning the sprout end of the corn upward, with the point of your knife take the back part of the husk off from it, and yet leaving a kind of husk on the
5 corn, or else it is marr'd; and then cut off that sprouted end (I mean a little of it) that the white may appear, and so pull off the husk on the cloven side (as I directed you) and then cutting off a very little of the other end, that so your hook may enter, and if your hook be small and good, you will find this to be a very
10 choice bait either for Winter or Summer, you sometimes casting a little of it into the place where your flote swims.

And to take the *Roch* and *Dace*, a good bait is the young brood of Wasps or Bees, baked or hardned in their husks in an Oven, after the bread is taken out of it, or on a fire-shovel; and so also
15 is the thick blood of *Sheep*, being halfe dryed on a trencher that you cut it into such pieces as may best fit the size of your hook, and a little salt keeps it from growing black, and makes it not the worse but better; this is taken to be a choice bait, if rightly ordered.

There be several Oiles of a strong smel that I have been told
20 of, and to be excellent to tempt fish to bite, of which I could say much, but I remember I once carried a small bottle from Sir *George Hastings* to Sir *Henry Wotton* (they were both chimical men) as a great present; but upon enquiry, I found it did not answer the expectation of Sir *Henry*, which with the help of other circum-
25 stances, makes me have little belief in such things as many men talk of; not but that I think fishes both smell and hear (as I have exprest in my former discourse) but there is a mysterious knack, which (though it be much easier then the Philosophers-Stone, yet) is not attainable by common capacities, or else lies locked up in
30 the braine or brest of some chimical men, that, like the *Rosi-crutions*, yet will not reveal it. But I stepped by chance into this discourse of Oiles, and fishes smelling; and though there might be more said, both of it, and of baits for *Roch* and *Dace*, and other flote fish, yet I will forbear it at this time, and tell you in the next place how
35 you are to prepare your tackling: concerning which I will for sport sake give you an old Rhime out of an old Fish-book, which will be a part of what you are to provide.

My rod, and my line, my flote and my lead,
My hook, and my plummet, my whetstone and knife,
My Basket, my baits, both living and dead,
My net, and my meat, for that is the chief;
Then I must have thred and hairs great and smal, 5
With mine Angling purse, and so you have all.

But you must have all these tackling, and twice so many more, with which, if you mean to be a fisher, you must store your selfe: and to that purpose I will go with you either to *Charles Brandons* (neer to the *Swan* in *Golding-lane*); or to Mr *Fletchers* in the Court 10 which did once belong to Dr *Nowel* the Dean of *Pauls*, that I told you was a good man, and a good Fisher; it is hard by the west end of Saint *Pauls* Church; they be both honest men, and will fit an Angler with what tackling hee wants.

Viat. Then, good Master, let it be at *Charles Brandons*, for he is 15 neerest to my dwelling, and I pray lets meet there the ninth of *May* next about two of the Clock, and I'l want nothing that a Fisher should be furnish'd with.

Pisc. Well, and Ile not fail you, God willing, at the time and place appointed. 20

Viat. I thank you, good Master, and I will not fail you: and good Master, tell me what baits more you remember, for it wil not now be long ere we shal be at *Totenham High-Cross*, and when we come thither, I wil make you some requital of your pains, by repeating as choice a copy of Verses, as any we have heard since 25 we met together, and that is a proud word; for wee have heard very good ones.

Pisc. Wel, Scholer, and I shal be right glad to hear them; and I wil tel you whatsoever comes in my mind, that I think may be worth your hearing: you may make another choice bait thus, Take 30 a handful or two of the best and biggest *Wheat* you can get, boil it in a little milk like as Frumitie is boiled, boil it so till it be soft, and then fry it very leisurely with honey, and a little beaten *Saffron* dissolved in milk, and you wil find this a choice bait, and good I think for any fish, especially for *Roch, Dace, Chub* or 35 *Greyling*; I know not but that it may be as good for a River *Carp*, and especially if the ground be a little baited with it.

You are also to know, that there be divers kind of *Cadis*, or *Case-worms*, that are to bee found in this Nation in several distinct Counties, and in several little Brooks that relate to bigger Rivers, as namely one *Cadis* called a *Piper*, whose husk or case is a piece
5 of reed about an inch long or longer, and as big about as the compass of a two pence; these worms being kept three or four days in a woollen bag with sand at the bottom of it, and the bag wet once a day, will in three or four dayes turne to be yellow; and these be a choice bait for the *Chub* or *Chavender*, or indeed for any
10 great fish, for it is a large bait.

There is also a lesser *Cadis-worm*, called a *Cock-spur*, being in fashion like the spur of a Cock, sharp at one end, and the case or house in which this dwels is made of smal *husks* and *gravel*, and *slime*, most curiously made of these, even so as to be wondred at, but not
15 made by man (no more then the nest of a bird is): this a choice bait for any flote fish, it is much less then the *Piper Cadis*, and to be so ordered; and these may be so preserved ten, fifteen, or twentie dayes.

There is also another *Cadis* called by some a *Straw-worm*, and
20 by some a *Ruffe-coate*, whose house or case is made of little pieces of bents, and Rushes, and straws, and water weeds, and I know not what, which are so knit together with condens'd slime, that they stick up about her husk or case, not unlike the *bristles* of a *Hedg-hog*; these three *Cadis* are commonly taken in the beginning
25 of Summer, and are good indeed to take any kind of fish with flote or otherwise. I might tell you of many more, which, as these doe early, so those have their time of turning to be flies later in Summer; but I might lose my selfe, and tire you by such a discourse; I shall therefore but remember you, that to know these, and their several
30 kinds, and to what flies every particular *Cadis* turns, and then how to use them, first as they bee *Cadis*, and then as they be flies, is an Art, and an Art that every one that professes Angling is not capable of.

But let mee tell you, I have been much pleased to walk quietly
35 by a Brook with a little stick in my hand, with which I might easily take these, and consider the curiosity of their composure; and if you shall ever like to do so, then note, that your stick must be

cleft, or have a nick at one end of it, by which meanes you may with ease take many of them out of the water, before you have any occasion to use them. These, my honest Scholer, are some observations told to you as they now come suddenly into my memory, of which you may make some use: but for the practical part, it is that that makes an Angler; it is diligence, and observation, and practice that must do it.

CHAP. XIII.

Pisc. Well, Scholer, I have held you too long about these *Cadis*, and my spirits are almost spent, and so I doubt is your patience; but being we are now within sight of *Totenham*, where I first met
5 you, and where wee are to part, I will give you a little direction how to colour the hair of which you make your lines, for that is very needful to be known of an *Angler*; and also how to paint your rod, especially your top, for a right grown top is a choice Commoditie, and should be preserved from the water soking into it,
10 which makes it in wet weather to be heavy, and fish ill favouredly, and also to rot quickly.

Take a pint of strong Ale, half a pound of soot, and a like quantity of the juice of Walnut-tree leaves, and an equal quantitie of Allome, put these together into a pot, or pan, or pipkin, and boil them
15 half an hour, and having so done, let it cool, and being cold, put your hair into it, and there let it lye; it wil turn your hair to be a kind of water, or glass colour, or greenish; and the longer you let it lye, the deeper coloured it will bee; you might be taught to make many other colours, but it is to little purpose; for doubtlesse
20 the water or glass coloured haire is the most choice and most useful for an *Angler*.

But if you desire to colour haire green, then doe it thus: Take a quart of smal Ale, halfe a pound of Allome, then put these into a pan or pipkin, and your haire into it with them, then put it upon
25 a fire and let it boile softly for half an hour, and then take out your hair, and let it dry; and having so done, then take a pottle of water, and put into it two handful of Mary-golds, and cover it with a tile or what you think fit, and set it again on the fire, where it is to boil softly for half an hour, about which time the
30 scum will turn yellow; then put into it half a pound of Copporis beaten smal, and with it the hair that you intend to colour, then let the hair be boiled softly till half the liquor be wasted, and then let it cool three or four hours with your hair in it; and you are to

observe, that the more *Copporis* you put into it, the greener it will be, but doubtless the pale green is best; but if you desire yellow hair (which is only good when the weeds rot) then put in the more *Mary-golds*, and abate most of the *Copporis*, or leave it out, and take a little Verdigreece in stead of it. 5

This for colouring your hair. And as for painting your rod, which must be in Oyl, you must first make a size with glue and water, boiled together until the glue be dissolved, and the size of a lie colour; then strike your size upon the wood with a bristle brush or pensil, whilst it is hot: that being quite dry, take white lead, 10 and a little red lead, and a little cole black, so much as all together will make an ash colour, grind these all together with Linseed oyle, let it be thick, and lay it thin upon the wood with a brush or pensil; this do for the ground of any colour to lie upon wood.

For a Green. 15

Take Pink and Verdigreece, and grind them together in Linseed oyl, as thick as you can well grind it, then lay it smoothly on with your brush, and drive it thin; once doing for the most part will serve, if you lay it wel, and be sure your first colour be throughly dry, before you lay on a second. 20

Well Scholer, you now see *Totenham*, and I am weary, and therefore glad that we are so near it; but if I were to walk many more dayes with you, I could stil be telling you more and more of the mysterious Art of Angling; but I wil hope for another opportunitie, and then I wil acquaint you with many more, both neces- 25 sary and true observations concerning fish and fishing: but now no more, lets turn into yonder Arbour, for it is a cleane and cool place.

Viat. 'Tis a faire motion, and I will requite a part of your courtesies with a bottle of *Sack*, and *Milk*, and *Oranges* and *Sugar*, which 30 all put together, make a drink too good for any body, but us Anglers: and so Master, here is a full glass to you of that liquor, and when you have pledged me, I wil repeat the Verses which I promised you; it is a Copy printed amongst Sir *Henry Wottons* Verses, and doubtless made either by him, or by a lover of Angling: Come 35

Master, now drink a glass to me, and then I will pledge you, and fall to my repetition; it is a discription of such Country recreations as I have enjoyed since I had the happiness to fall into your company.

5
Quivering fears, heart tearing cares,
Anxious sighes, untimely tears,
   Fly, fly to Courts,
   Fly to fond wordlings sports,
Where strain'd Sardonick smiles are glosing stil
10
And grief is forc'd to laugh against her will.
   Where mirths but Mummery,
   And sorrows only real be.

Fly from our Country pastimes, fly,
Sad troops of humane misery,
15
   Come serene looks,
   Clear as the Christal Brooks,
Or the pure azur'd heaven that smiles to see
The Rich attendance on our poverty;
   Peace and a secure mind
20
   Which all men seek, we only find.

Abused Mortals did you know
Where joy, hearts ease, and comforts grow,
   You'd scorn proud Towers,
   And seek them in these Bowers,
25
Where winds sometimes our woods perhaps may shake,
But blustering care could never tempest make,
   No murmurs ere come nigh us,
   Saving of Fountains that glide by us.

Here's no fantastick Mask nor Dance,
30
But of our kids that frisk and prance;
   Nor wars are seen
   Unless upon the green
Two harmless Lambs are butting one the other,
Which done, both bleating, run each to his mother:
35
   And wounds are never found,
   Save what the Plough-share gives the ground.

Here are no false entrapping baits
To hasten too too hasty fates;

Unless it be
the fond credulitie
Of silly fish, which, worlding like, still look
Upon the bait, but never on the hook;
Nor envy, 'nless among   5
The birds, for price of their sweet Song.

Go, let the diving Negro *seek*
For gems hid in some forlorn creek,
We all Pearls scorn,
Save what the dewy morne   10
Congeals upon each little spire of grasse,
Which careless Shepherds beat down as they passe,
And Gold ne're here appears
Save what the yellow Ceres *bears.*

Blest silent Groves, oh may you be   15
For ever mirths best nursery,
May pure contents
for ever pitch their tents
Upon these downs, these Meads, these rocks, these mountains,
And peace stil slumber by these purling fountains   20
Which we may every year
find when we come a fishing here.

Pisc. Trust me, Scholer, I thank you heartily for these Verses,
they be choicely good, and doubtless made by a lover of Angling:
Come, now drink a glass to me, and I wil requite you with a very   25
good Copy of Verses; it is a farewel to the vanities of the world,
and some say written by *Dr. D*, but let them bee writ by whom
they will, he that writ them had a brave soul, and must needs be
possest with happy thoughts at the time of their composure.

Farwel ye guilded follies, pleasing troubles,   30
Farwel ye honour'd rags, ye glorious bubbles,
Fame's but a hollow eccho, gold pure clay,
Honour the darling but of one short day.
Beauty (th'eyes idol) but a damask'd skin,
State but a golden prison, to live in   35
And torture free-born minds; imbroider'd trains
Meerly but Pageants, for proud swelling vains,

And blood ally'd to greatness, is alone
Inherited, not purchas'd, nor our own.
   Fame, honor, beauty, state, train, blood and birth,
   Are but the fading blossoms of the earth.

5   I would be great, but that the Sun doth still,
Level his rayes against the rising hill:
I would be high, but see the proudest Oak
Most subject to the rending Thunder-stroke;
I would be rich, but see men too unkind
10   Dig in the bowels of the richest mind;
I would be wise, but that I often see
The Fox suspected whilst the Ass goes free;
I would be fair, but see the fair and proud
Like the bright Sun, oft setting in a cloud;
15   I would be poor, but know the humble grass
Still trampled on by each unworthy Asse:
Rich, hated; wise, suspected; scorn'd, if poor;
Great, fear'd; fair, tempted; high, stil envi'd more:
   I have wish'd all, but now I wish for neither,
20   Great, high, rich, wise, nor fair, poor I'l be rather.

Would the world now adopt me for her heir,
Would beauties Queen entitle me the Fair,
Fame speak me fortunes Minion, could I vie
Angels with India, with a speaking eye
25   Command bare heads, bow'd knees, strike Justice dumb
As wel as blind and lame, or give a tongue
To stones, by Epitaphs, be call'd great Master,
In the loose Rhimes of every Poetaster;
Could I be more then any man that lives,
30   Great, fair, rich, wise, in all Superlatives.
Yet I more freely would these gifts resign,
Then ever fortune would have made them mine
   And hold one minute of this holy leasure,
   Beyond the riches of this empty pleasure.

35   Welcom pure thoughts, welcome ye silent groves,
These guests, these Courts, my soul most dearly loves:
Now the wing'd people of the Skie shall sing
My cheerful Anthems to the gladsome Spring;

A Pray'r book now shall be my looking glasse,
In which I will adore sweet vertues face.
Here dwell no hateful looks, no Pallace cares,
No broken vows dwell here, nor pale fac'd fears,
Then here I'l sit and sigh my hot loves folly,   5
   And learn t'affect an holy melancholy.
    And if contentment be a stranger, then
    I'l nere look for it, but in heaven again.

Viat. Wel Master, these be Verses that be worthy to keep a room
in every mans memory. I thank you for them, and I thank you   10
for your many instructions, which I will not forget; your company
and discourse have been so pleasant, that I may truly say, I have
only lived, since I enjoyed you and them, and turned Angler. I
am sorry to part with you here, here in this place where I first
met you, but it must be so: I shall long for the ninth of *May*, for   15
then we are to meet at *Charls Brandons.* This intermitted time wil
seem to me (as it does to men in sorrow) to pass slowly, but I
wil hasten it as fast as I can by my wishes, and in the mean time
the blessing of Saint Peters *Master be with mine.*

Pisc. And the like be upon my honest Scholer. And upon all   20
that hate contentions, and love *quietnesse,* and *vertue,* and *Angling.*

FINIS.

APPENDIX

The Angler's Song

The music and words for the bass part on the pages reproduced overleaf were inverted to enable the two singers to read their parts at the same time.

(216)

The ANGLERS Song.

For two Voyces, Treble and Basse.   C A N T V S.   Mr. Henry Lawes.

Man's life is but vain; for 'tis subject to pain, and sorrow,

… short as a buble; 'tis a hodge podge of businefs, and mony, and

care, and care, and mony, and trouble. But we'l take no care when the

weather proves fair, nor will we vex now though it rain; we'l banifh

all forrow, and fing till to morrow, and Angle, and Angle again.

Postscript by

Lord Home

No fish, however aristocratic or however coarse, could wish for a doughtier champion than Izaak Walton. He is totally and gloriously biased. Water – because it harbours the fishes – is the best of the elements, with earth and air running a poor second and third. The Bible and the Classics – prose and poetry – are combed for quotations to justify that assertion, and all the resources of theology and learning are called in aid. To emphasize the impeccable ancestry of the angler Seth, the son of Adam is said to have been a master of the arts of fishing; Job and Amos had both mentioned fish-hooks in their writings; while Peter, Andrew and John were selected to witness the Transfiguration because they were fishermen. The ultimate in perfection was the Flood. So from Noah to Sir Henry Wotton, Provost of Eton and Walton's friend, a fisherman could do no ill.

Angling was an art, and a hobby fit for gentlemen. Walton described it as 'humble, calm, quiet and educational'.

> *Let me live harmlessly, and near the brink*
> *Of* Trent *or* Avon *have a dwelling place.*

But Walton was not a fishing snob, nor, in the modern jargon, a purist. For he gives quite as much attention to the common chub as he does to the lordly salmon. That he looks forward to cooking the fish before it is caught is simply the measure of his confidence in his skill. For he is sure not only that he can hook and land his chub, but that from a shoal he can select the individual of his choice. The secret is to balance the rod on the branch of a tree overhanging a deep pool, and to dangle the hook a quarter of a yard (no more and no less) above the surface of the water. The hook is baited with a live green grasshopper. During these preliminary manoeuvres the chub will have moved to the river bottom, but they will rise to the surface when all is quiet. That is the signal to lower the point of the rod, 'as softly as a Snail moves', until the tantalizing lure is placed so close in front of the mouth of the intended victim that it is irresistible. Q.E.D! for all these instructions are valid today.

So we graduate up the fishes' social ladder to the trout – in Walton's words a 'generous' fish and dainty to the palate. He sought them in the rivers of the south of England, the Dove in Derbyshire being the northern limit of the area with which he was intimately acquainted. He knew all about the east winds of March, but his joy was in the meadows in April, May and June, when nature is at its most beautiful. He would embrace it all – the sky, the trees, the flora and fauna and the milkmaid.

> *Come live with me, and be my Love,*
> *And we wil all the pleasures prove,*
>
> *By shallow River, to whose falls*
> *Mellodious birds sing madrigals*
>
> *If these delights thy mind may move,*
> *Then live with me, and be my Love.*

In the taking of the trout Piscator proves himself once again to be no purist, for his first lesson concerns angling with the worm and the minnow, which would today be judged the lowest forms of the art. First dig for your worms when the soil is damp and soft. Use the lobworm if possible, and then preserve them in moss or fennel to toughen them for the hook. This is fundamental to worm-fishing, as there is nothing more frustrating than the frequent fracture of fresh worms. And, should the worms malinger, feed them on a little milk or cream and add for good measure some egg, beaten and boiled. Times have changed for the worse!

But his seventeenth-century recipe for bringing worms to the surface when the earth is hard and dry is in essence the same: 'Squeeze almond leaves with water and salt, and pour the mixture onto the surface of the ground.' The modern way is a tablespoon of mustard to a tumbler of water, but either will work. So, too, the instructions for placing the hook in the worms to the best advantage, so that it does not catch in every tuft of grass. So, too, the threading of the gut and hook through the gills of a minnow, so that it will 'turn the better' when it is pulled across and against the stream. They all apply to modern angling. Even in those early days there was an artificial minnow made of silk with suitable stuffing, but then as now the 'natural' for trout produced the best results. Somehow the mechanical spin is too fast and too straight, and fails to give that darting, glinting effect which in a dark water is virtually irresistible to the big brown trout. Walton does not, however, mention fishing the upstream worm or minnow, which in fast-running water can be so deadly to the brown trout in the month of June, and which – set racing at full speed down the current – will bring the salmon chasing it as far as the fisherman's feet.

But Piscator knew all about the larvae and pupae which would later hatch into the flies and insects on which the fish would feed. He was a meticulous observer, and his accounts of the caterpillars of the privet hawk moth and the puss moth are so accurate as to need no illustrations. Occasionally they would fall from the bushes into the stream, or a field-mouse would fail to make the opposite bank, and then the cannibal trout or the pike would enjoy a bonus meal.

It is intriguing to compare the flies with which they fished with those in a modern catalogue. To them the march brown of today was the bright brown (with the hair of an aborted calf and a brown hen's wing); the green drake and the grey drake (which names are still used) are the may-fly. The little black gnat (the body as little as you can possibly make it and the wings as short as the body), the turkey fly and the yellow dun are easily identifiable. For the whirling blue dun there were two dressings. The first, the fur from the bottom of a squirrel's tail, with the wing the grey feather of a mallard drake; the second, and the most killing, the down of a fox cub, ribbed with yellow silk and the mallard wing. It is possible, too, to identify the red spinner, and the iron blue, the cow dung fly (the cow turd fly) and quite a number more with reasonable accuracy.

Walton accepted the specification given by Thomas Barker for the ideal trout-rod. It ought to be two-piece and of a balance answering to the word 'gentle'. Of course the anglers of that day knew nothing of such luxuries as split-cane, or fibre-glass, or carbon-fibre,

which cater for shortness and lightness and extra power. They therefore fished with longer rods, but they were finely made. I recall
with affection a salmon-rod with which I started as a teenage boy.
It was twenty-two feet long, but in a stiff wind it 'did it all', and
for large autumn salmon it was a more than adequate match.
Walton and his friends fished with hair, varying its strength by
reducing the numbers needed to one hair's breadth when the baro-
meter was set fair and the sky was blue. It is still our practice with
gut to change down from 1 × to 3 or 4 × and to use tea or the
juice of vegetable dye to reduce its visibility. What a wealth of
discussion would have been provoked had the dry fly been in vogue,
although Piscator had the essence of it in his instruction to the
learners to let the trout turn its head down into the stream before
the strike was made.

He had much more advice to give to his companion.

> When the winde is south,
> It blows your bait into a fishes mouth.

Let that wind if at all possible be behind the angler. All these
precepts were true, although it must be said that a large part of
Piscator's teaching was catching the trout. And poor Viator,
guilty of clumsily losing a fish, is told in no uncertain terms that,
had his mentor been holding the rod, the great trout would not
have got away, but would have succumbed to the correct strain
of rod and line as it fought against man and the stream.

When he comes to the salmon, described by Walton as 'The King
of the Fishes', the reader will be surprised that his discourse
on it is so short as to be almost abrupt. The explanation is that
he did not practise his art on the great rivers of Scotland and Wales.
There were, it is true, salmon in the Thames in those days, but
he seemed to prefer the sport given in the smaller and quieter waters
of the streams. But he does mark one contrast between then and
now; for he named summer as the season of the salmon's run from
the sea, and August as the time of spawning. There are a few rivers
in Scotland where that is still so, but the trend has been for the
summer run to start later and later until, on some of the main
rivers, the closing date in October seems to come too soon.

The reason is not far to seek. Draining in the hills is now so much more extensive that rainwater is taken off the land a great deal faster than it used to be. Rivers in summer are therefore lower than they were in Walton's day. In 1836, the Lord Home of the day, who fished the Tweed, landed a hundred heavy fish in a week, and yet noted that the floods were running off much more quickly than they had done when he was young. He wrote: 'It is the difference between a roof which is tiled and one which is thatched. From the former the water will run off in a day, while from the latter it will drip for a week.' So the fish have adapted themselves to the new conditions, and run in early spring and late in autumn; the exceptions are short rivers and those which are fed by melting snows into the summer months. Walton declares that the salmon, the further they travel from the sea, become both fatter and better. Fatter – yes; better – no, for the fat is spawn and the flesh is flabby.

There is another interesting contrast between Walton's day and ours. If any modern fisherman were asked to name the lure most likely to catch the salmon he would not select the lobworm even if it was 'anointed with . . . the oil of Ivy-berries'. Now the selection would be a fly (with a sunk or floating line), or a spinning minnow, sprat or spoon, with a marked preference for the fly-fishing which is the highest form of the art.

Can salmon and trout smell? Walton is not alone in suggesting it. There has long been a belief handed down by fishermen on the Tweed that the heron secretes an oil in its thighs which attracts the trout within range of his bill. Certainly the heron when he is looking for his meal stands still, which is a lesson which many a fisherman could learn to advantage.

Anyhow, Piscator, while paying homage to the salmon, reverts with comparative delight to the fish which inhabit the slow and gliding waters. He starts with the tyrannical pike, with jaws so strong and teeth so sharp that they can mangle a human limb. It is in character that the pike prefers a live bait, and Piscator gives minute instructions on how to thread the line and the hook through the skin of the back of a roach or a bream, or through the gills of the luckless frog. The modern way is with a wire trace and most commonly a spoon. I once caught a giant pike with a gut cast.

I was returning from salmon fishing and had an old No. 6. salmon fly (a Wilkinson) on the end of my cast. I threw it idly into the lake as I passed by and the result was a monster of 27 lb. The fly was so firmly in the corner of its jaws that it could not bring its teeth into play. As is the pike's habit it made three long runs and then abruptly surrendered.

The Pike is so ruthless a killer (he will wipe out a brood of wild duck with delight) that almost any method to get rid of him is held to be justifiable. One such is to attach the line with the live bait to floating bales of straw or empty bottles or pieces of wood and to launch them onto the lake or pond on a still night. The pike, played by an invisible and tireless opponent, will wear himself out and is easily taken. It redeems its reputation to some extent when it is cooked by a really good chef. The Polish Armoured Division, when they were quartered in Scotland during the War, made them reasonably edible. But they had to do without the thyme, sweet marjoram, winter savory, mace and claret which Piscator insisted were necessary to render the fish palatable.

And so to the carp, which Walton named 'The Queen of the Rivers', although that is a little flattering as they are neither slim nor elegant. Piscator calls it the most subtle of all the fishes and most anglers would agree with that compliment for it is undeniably hard to catch. They were early in the fish-ponds of Britain, the nearest clue to the date of their introduction being indicated in the doggerel:

Hops and Turkies, Carps and Beer
Came into England all in a year.

More accurately the carp should be called 'The Queen of the Ponds' for it is essentially a denizen of their deep and still waters. Piscator recommends as the best bait the blueish marsh or meadow worm or paste, insisting that ground-bait freely scattered before the fishing day will greatly aid the chance of a catch, and he gives a recipe for the chosen day: 'Take the flesh of Rabet cut smal', with flour, sugar and honey added, or if the bait is 'Gentles' add 'a small piece of scarlet'. He is so meticulous that the size is drawn thus ■ in the text of *The Compleat Angler*. All this, however, will be of no avail unless the fisherman has endless patience, is quiet and has a light hand.

Discourse is always followed by verse and song, praising the virtue of even the smallest sprat and those who fish in the water.

> *Oh the brave Fishers life,*
> *It is the best of any,*
> *'Tis full of pleasure, void of strife,*
> *And 'tis belov'd of many:*
> > *Other joyes*
> > *are but toyes,*
> > *only this*
> > *lawful is,*
> > *for our skil*
> > *breeds no ill,*
> *but content and pleasure.*

That, of course, was the secret. Everything in nature subscribed to Izaak Walton's content, and angling capped the lot. In *The Compleat Angler* all this love of fishing and nature comes pouring out to the captive and enthralled reader.

Even so, the wonder of it is that this man was born in the Black Country, apprenticed to a Whitehall haberdasher, and described in 1626 as a 'City of London Ironmonger'. He married, it is true, into the Church, and had the run of the bishoprics and vicarages in England, which were apt to be pastoral places. True, too, that the company of his choice was that of scholars, divines and theologians whose conversation was cultured and high-minded and clear in exposition and argument. Nevertheless, Walton's mellifluous prose was recognizably his own, and ensured that his wide and meticulous knowledge of fishing, so clearly expressed, would qualify as a classic. It is still so. After 300 years the Angler's Song is still the heart and soul of the matter.

> *But we'll take no care*
> *When the weather proves fair*
> *Nor will we vex now, though it rain;*
> *We'll banish all sorrow*
> *And sing till to morrow,*
> *And Angle and Angle again.*

NOTES

These are intended primarily to clarify the meaning of the text, and bibliographic references have been kept to a minimum. Readers interested in a fuller account of the sources and analogues for Walton's ideas are advised to consult Jonquil Bevan's edition of *The Compleat Angler* (Oxford, 1983).

ABBREVIATIONS USED IN THE NOTES

DNB   *Dictionary of National Biography.*

Dubartas   *The Divine Weeks and Works of Guillaume De Saluste, sieur Du Bartas*, trans. Joshua Sylvester, ed. S. Snyder (Oxford, 1979).

OED   *Oxford English Dictionary.*

Tilley   M. P. Tilley, *A Dictionary of the Proverbs in England in the Sixteenth and Seventeenth Centuries* (Ann Arbor, 1950).

NOTES TO THE EDITOR'S INTRODUCTION

1. His date of birth is traditionally ascribed to 9 August, the day on which he began to write his will in his ninetieth year.
2. See '*The copy of a Letter writ to* Mr Izaak Walton, *by Doctor* King *Lord Bishop* of Chichester', in *The Lives of John Donne, Sir Henry Wotton, Richard Hooker, George Herbert and Robert Sanderson*, ed. George Saintsbury (Oxford, 1927; reprinted 1973), p. 15. All references to Walton's *Lives* are to this edition.
3. *Lives*, p. 21.
4. ibid., p. 84.
5. ibid., p. 371.
6. Cited by John R. Cooper in his *The Art of the Compleat Angler* (Durham, N.C., 1968), p. 23.
7. *Lives*, p. 379.
8. ibid., p. 143.
9. See B. D. Greenslade, '*The Compleat Angler* and the sequestered Clergy', *RES*, 2nd series, V (1954), pp. 361–6.
10. *The Compleat Angler*, p. 25. All references are to this edition, unless otherwise stated.
11. ibid., p. 24.
12. My argument is indebted to John R. Cooper's pioneering study (see above). In particular, see pp. 30–77.
13. John Chalker, *The English Georgic* (London, 1969), p. 10.
14. *The Compleat Angler*, p. 123.
15. William Cowper, *The Task*.

16. Pastoral is a contested term which has been applied to a bewildering variety of works. For a more comprehensive discussion see the Introduction in Bryan Loughrey (ed.), *The Pastoral Mode* (London and Basingstoke, 1984).
17. *The Compleat Angler*, pp. 47–8.
18. ibid., pp. 71–2: 'and sate as quietly and as free from cares under this *Sycamore*, as *Virgils Tityrus* and his *Meliboeus* did under their broad *Beech* tree'.
19. ibid., p. 24.
20. ibid., p. 29.
21. Jonquil Bevan's edition of *The Compleat Angler* provides a valuable critical apparatus designed to show how the book developed.
22. Bevan, p. 181.
23. In the 'biological Memoir' prefixed to his edition of *The Compleat Angler* (1836). Cited in Bevan, p. 13.

NOTES TO THE TITLE PAGE

Simon Peter said . . .: John 21:3. The Authorized Version reads: 'Simon Peter saith unto them, I go afishing, they say unto him, we also go with thee.'

NOTES TO THE TEXT (line references at left)

Page 17
23 *curiositie*: pursuit or hobby.
26 *Sir Henry Wotton*: Sir Henry Wotton (1568–1639), diplomat, Provost of Eton College, poet and art connoisseur. Walton edited his papers, *Reliquiae Wottonianae* (1651), and prefixed to them his *Life of Wotton*.

Page 18
3 *exceptions*: objections.

Page 19
17 *sowr complexioned*: complexion here refers to the temperament or disposition.
22 *honest Nat. and R.R.*: Nat. and R. Roe were probably relatives of Walton.
24 *pictures of the Trout*: the identity of the artist is unknown.

Page 20
6 *Hales*: George Hale, *The private Schoole of defence* (1614).
15 *conference*: collection.
33 *that the east wind may never blow* . . .: proverbial. Cf. Tilley, W 442: 'When the wind is in the east it is good for neither man nor beast.'

CHAPTER I
Page 23
6 *Piscator*: Latin for angler.
7 *Viator*: Latin for traveller.

9–15 Piscator and Viator travel north along the road following the Lea valley from Tottenham to Ware. The Thatched House was an inn which stood near Hoddesdon High Street.

23 *Good company makes the way seem shorter*: it is unclear why Walton attributes this proverb to the Italians. Cf. Tilley, C 566: 'Good company makes short miles.'

Page 24

6 *Mr* ————: later editions identify Ralph Sadler (d. 1660) of Standon.

14 *very breed*: entire species.

28 *pleasant*: jocular or facetious.

Page 25

3–10 An extremely loose rendering of a passage from Michel de Montaigne's 'An Apologie of Raymond Sebond' possibly based on notes taken from John Florio's translation of Montaigne's *Essayes* (1603): 'When I am playing with my Cat, who knowes whether she have more sport in dallying with me, than I have in gaming with her? We entertaine one another with mutuall apish trickes. If I have my houre to begin or refuse, so hath she hers.'

17 *Lucian*: Greek satirist (*c.* A.D. 120–*c.* A.D. 180).

21–4 The epigram is significantly adapted from that prefixed to *Certaine Select Dialogues of Lucian*, trans. Francis Hickes (Oxford, 1634).

> Lucian well skill'd in old toyes this hath writ:
>> For all's but folly that men thinke is witt:
> No settled judgement doth in men appeare;
>> But thou admirest that which others jeere.

25 *Solomon sayes*: Proverbs 24 : 9: 'and the scorner is an abomination to men'.

Page 27

3 *Vertue, a reward to it self*: proverbial. Cf. Tilley, V 81: 'Virtue is its own reward.'

9 *Deucalions Floud*: in Greek mythology Deucalion, the son of Prometheus, and his wife, Phyrra, were the only survivors of the great Flood. They repopulated the earth by casting stones over their shoulders. Those thrown by Deucalion became men; those thrown by Phyrra, women. John Dennys's *The Secrets of Angling* (1613) describes how Deucalion then invented angling in order to feed his extended family. In the marginal note Walton mistakenly attributed the work to 'J. Da.' (Jo. Davors).

10 *Belus*: in Greek mythology the son of Poseidon. Gervase Markham, in *The Pleasures of Princes* (1615), held that 'it is most certaine that both Ducallion, Saturne and Bellus are taken for figures of Noah and his family, and the invention of the Art of Angling is truely sayd to come from the sonnes of Seth'.

13 *Seth*: Adam's third son. His descendants were believed to have inscribed knowledge of the arts and sciences on stone pillars which survived the Flood.

23 *Amos*: Amos 4:2.

24 *Job*: Job 41:1, 2.

25 *Moses*: the view that Moses wrote the Book of Job was eccentric even in the seventeenth century.

Page 28

3 *accidental*: incidental.

34 *humane*: a common spelling of human.

Page 29

14 *ingenuous Spaniard*: cannot be identified.

24 ff. Walton would have found reference to most of these wonders in Dubartas, the Third Day of the First Week, ll. 235 72.

27 *Camden*: William Camden (1551 1623), antiquarian and author of *Britannia* (1586), the first comprehensive topographical survey of England. Walton elsewhere refers to him as Cambden.

30 Walton's reference to Aristotle as the source of this legend is incorrect.

34 *Josephus*: Flavius Josephus (c. A.D. 37 -c. A.D. 100), Jewish theologian and historian.

Page 30

4 15 Stanzas 36, 8 and 7 (with some slight amendments) of Herbert's 'Providence'.

21 *Pliny*: Pliny the Elder (A.D. 23–79) was considered an authority on scientific matters during the Middle Ages and the Renaissance. Walton quotes his *Natural History*, trans. Philemon Holland (1601).

24 *Gesner*: Conrad von Gesner (1516–65) wrote a number of works on natural history. Walton generally refers to *Historia Animalium* (1558).
Randelitius: Guillaume Rondelet (1507 66), author of *De Piscibus Marinis* (1555).

26 *Dubartas*: Guillaume de Saluste, sieur du Bartas (1544 90). His Protestant epic on the theme of the Creation was translated by Joshua Sylvester as *Du Bartas His Devine Weekes and Workes* (1611). The passage follows, not totally accurately, the Fifth Day of the First Week, 30 48.

29 30 The belief that the sea contained marine counterparts of all land creatures was a seventeenth-century commonplace.

33 *Stares*: starlings.

Page 31

16 *Cuttle-fish*: Walton takes his description of the cuttle-fish from Montaigne's 'An Apologie of Raymond Sebond'. However, Montaigne had confused the cuttle-fish with the angler-fish.

26 *Sargus*: the sea-bream.

32 ff. Dubartas, Fifth Day of First Week, ll. 196 200.

Page 32

3 *Cantharus*: the black sea-bream.

5–8 Dubartas, Fifth Day of First Week, ll. 201–4.

19 *Rarity*: the original reads 'Variety'. Although this makes sense all sub-sequent editions substitute 'Rarity'. Possibly 'Variety' was a printer's misreading of 'Rariety', an obsolete form of 'Rarity'.

27–30 Dubartas, Fifth Day of First Week, ll. 205–8.

28 *pheer*: mate.

34 *sensless*: without feelings.

Page 33

1 *considerable*: worthy to be considered.

5 6 *example of tender affection*: Matthew 23:37.

8 *flags*: flat stones.

Page 34

4 Matthew 10:2.

6 *Transfiguration*: Matthew 17:1 8.

11 *ingenous and learned man*: almost certainly John Donne (1572 1631), poet and Dean of St Paul's. Walton's *Life of Donne* was published with Donne's sermons in 1640. Walton probably refers to Donne's sermon preached to Queen Anne (14 December 1617).

17 *Love-Song betwixt God and his Church*: the Canticles or Song of Solomon.

35 *Doctor Nowel*: Dr Alexander Nowell (c. 1507 1602). His 'Small Catechism' (instructions in the elements of Christian faith set out in the form of question and answer), inserted before the order of confirmation in the *Prayer Book* of 1549 and supplemented in 1604, remains the official Anglican catechism.

Page 35

25 *Sir Henry Wotton*: see notes to p. 17 above.

Page 36

10–33 This is adapted from the poem 'On a Banck as I sate a fishing, A description of the spring' in *Reliquiae Wottonianae* (1651).

19 *swift Pilgrims*: house-martins.

21 *Philomel*: the nightingale.

27 *Sillibub*: sillabub. A drink made of milk or cream curdled with wine or cider.

35 *another Angler*: in his marginal note Walton ascribes the poem which follows to 'Jo. Da.' (Jo. Davors). In fact, the quotation comes from John Dennys, *The Secrets of Angling* (1613), although Walton has made considerable alterations.

Page 37

16 *ganderglass*: ragwort.

16 *Culverkayes*: in the seventeenth century the term applied to the wild hyacinth or bluebell.

20–24 In Greek mythology Aurora was the goddess of the dawn and Tithonus her husband.

27 *vains*: defined in the *OED* as 'rivulet', but the sense here requires 'watershed'.

37 *Flora*: the goddess of flowers.

CHAPTER 2
Page 39

4 *put down*: a technical term in hunting. To cause a fish or beast to swim low in the water.

6 *Lady-smocks*: cuckoo-flowers.

10 *complement*: exchange greetings.

26 *pleasant*: amusing.

Page 40

3 *Falling-sickness*: epilepsy.

4 *Benione*: benzion, 'the frankincense of Java', an aromatic resin.

8 *vent*: surfacing to breathe.

26 *ingenuous Gentleman*: Walton's marginal note names Mr Nich. Seagrave. He cannot, however, be identified with any certainty.

30 *Old Rose*: title of a popular ballad.

Page 41

20 *Trout-Hal*: they later change their plans and stay instead at Bleak Hall.

26 *the Poet*: cannot be identified, but possibly Walton himself.

Page 42

31–2 *conveniently*: becomingly.

Page 44

3 *soaring*: remaining at the surface.

18 *towardly*: apt.

28 *Gentle*: maggot.
Cod-worm: larva of the caddis-fly.

35 *bit*: bite.

Page 46

11 *sippets*: fragments.

33 *sleight*: skill.

Page 47

6 *Catch*: a round in which one singer catches at the words of another, producing ludicrous effects.

22 ff. For a discussion of the conscious pastoralism of this passage, see above, pp. 10–11.

34 *Poet*: again, cannot be identified but possibly refers to Walton himself.

Page 48
32 ff. Christopher Marlowe's 'Come live with me' first appeared in the *Passionate Pilgrim* (1599), and with additional stanzas in *England's Helicon* (1600).

Page 49
6 *posies*: bouquets of flowers.

7 *Kirtle*: a gown or skirt.

22 *Sir Thomas Overbury*: Sir Thomas Overbury (1581–1613), poet, essayist and victim of a notorious intrigue at the court of James I. His *The Wife, with Additions of New Characters* (1622) contains a famous description of a milkmaid, whose only wish is that 'shee may die in the Spring-time, to have store of flowers stucke upon her winding sheet'.

25 *The Milk maids mothers answer*: first appeared in *England's Helicon* (1600), where it is given to 'Ignoto'. The attribution to Sir Walter Ralegh stems largely from Walton's statement in *The Compleat Angler*.

CHAPTER 3
Page 51
3 *cast*: decide.

6 *daping*: dapping. To fish by letting the bait bob on the surface of the water.

14 *like*: suitable.

Page 52
13–14 Cf. Matthew 13:3–9.

28–9 *'Tis merry in Hall when men sing all*: proverbial. Cf. Tilley, H 55: 'It is merry in Hall when beards wag all.'

31 *Mr William Basse*: William Basse (d. 1653?), a minor poet whose verses survive in manuscript collections.

Page 53
3 *Ketch*: catch or round. See notes to pp. 47 and 53.
against: before.

13 *Coridons Song*: John Chalkhill (c. 1590–1642) is the author. Walton edited his long poem *Thealma and Clearchus* (1683).

Page 54
2 *russet*: coarse cloth.

28 *roundelayes*: a song in which a line or refrain forms a recurrent motif.

Page 55
10–11 *'Tis the company and not the charge that makes the feast*: proverbial. Cf. Tilley, C 572: 'It is the company that makes the Feast.'

16 *The Anglers Song*: the author is William Basse. See notes to p. 52 above.

27 *fond*: foolish.

Page 56

20 *Fishers of men*: Matthew 4:19.

25–6 *last Food*: Luke 24:42.

34 *prevent*: anticipate.

Page 57

13 *against*: in readiness for.

29 *Lake Lemon*: Lake Leman.

31 *Mercator*: Gerhardus Mercator (1512 94), cartographer famous for the Mercator projection. Walton refers to his *Historia Mundi*, trans. W.S. (1635).

Page 58

3 *Winchester*: that is, the river Itchen.

4 *Skegger Trout*: immature salmon.

9 *Fordig Trout*: Fordwich is a village on the river Stour near Canterbury which is famous for its sea-trout.

14 *Sir George Hastings*: probably Sir George Hastings, son of the eccentric sportsman Henry Hastings. The *DNB* gives the date of his death as 1657, which conflicts with Walton's belief that he was 'now with God' when *The Compleat Angler* appeared in 1653.

22 *poriness*: the condition of being porous.

24 *he knowes his season*: Jeremiah 8:7.

28–35 Walton incorrectly ascribes this belief to Sir Francis Bacon.

35 *Albertus*: Albertus Magnus (*c.* 1200–1280), philosopher, theologian and natural historian. He was a prolific scholar, whose works were cited at length in Edward Topsell's *Historie of Serpents* (1608), the authority for most of Walton's observations concerning frogs.

Page 59

21 *Sir Francis Bacon*: Sir Francis Bacon (1561–1626), lawyer, philosopher, statesman and essayist. Walton here refers to his *History of Life and Death* (1638).

Page 60

20–21 *Palm trees*: could refer to several kinds of trees and shrubs, mainly of the willow family, which were substituted for true palms during the celebration of Palm Sunday.

CHAPTER 4
Page 61

3 *how to catch them*: Walton relies heavily on advice contained in Thomas Barker's *The Art of Angling* (1651).

19 *quick*: vigorous.

Page 62

24 *want*: lack.

Page 63

2 *Palmer flie or worm*: hairy caterpillars of migratory habits.

12 *Colworts*: any plant of the cabbage variety.

25 *curious*: assiduous.

Page 64

7 *this very description*: the description is taken from Topsell's *Historie of serpents*.

23 Dubartas, Sixth Day of First Week, ll. 1100–1120.

27 *Venus deed*: copulation.

28 *cold humour*: dampness.

33 *Fly Perausta*: mythological creature.

Page 65

1 *slow Boötes*: the Northern constellation of the Wagoner. In his marginal note Walton refers the reader to Gerard's *Herball* (1597).

17 *powdered Bief*: dried or salted beef.

Page 66

11 *Lecturer*: a clergyman appointed by the parish to preach sermons, but who did not bear the other responsibilities of a parish priest.

Page 67

3 *Thomas Barker*: author of *The Art of Angling* (1651). Little is known of his life, but he was probably a professional angler.

10 *haires*: fishing lines were made out of twisted horse hairs.

18 *amazes*: startles.

20 *March*: Walton employs the old calendar, so that all dates given are eleven days earlier than the modern calendar.

26 *arm*: attach the hook to the line.

36 *Crewel*: yarn.

Page 68

21 *sad*: dark.

26 *peckled*: speckled.

28 *hit*: succeed.

35 *Lapland*: famous for its witches.

Page 69

2 *smoaking*: smoking. The sense is obscure: either a heavy shower producing effects similar to fog, or a short shower which will be followed by sunshine and misty evaporations.

7 *South winde*: proverbial. See Tilley, W 443.

12 *Solomon observes*: Ecclesiastes 11:4.

16 *no good horse of a bad colour*: proverbial. Cf. Tilley, H 646: 'A good horse cannot be of a bad colour.'

24–5 *May-butter*: butter produced in May was particularly runny because the cows were feeding on new grass.

Page 70

21 *against*: before.

Page 71

3 *Sweet day, so cool, so calm, so bright*: the title of the poem is 'Vertue' and it first appeared in Herbert's *The Temple* (1633).

13 *closes*: the conclusion of a musical phrase, theme or movement; a cadence.

22 *which*: who.

35 *Virgil*: Virgil (Publius Vergilius Maro: 70–19 B.C.), the great Roman poet whose pastoral poem *The Eclogues* opens with Tityrus and Meliboeus in conversation beneath a beech tree.

Page 72

5 *Frank Davison*: Frank Davison (1575–c. 1619) published an anthology of verses, *A Poetical Rhapsody* (1602), which contained 'The Beggers Song'. However, the author was 'A.W.', whose identity remains unknown.

12 *clappers*: rattles employed by beggars to draw attention to themselves.

24 *A hundred herds of black and white*: fleas, etc.

Page 73

8 *ell*: a measurement of 45 inches.

20 *false quarter*: technical farrier's term for infirmity of the hoof.

CHAPTER 5
Page 74

10 *swift*: fast current.

Page 75

2 *Gesner*: see notes to p. 30 above.
   forty furlong: a furlong is a measurement of 220 yards.

3 *Francis Bacon*: the reference is to his *Natural History* (1626).

23 *Lemster*: Leominster was famous for its wool.

Page 76

1 *Every thing is beautifull in his season*: cf. Ecclesiastes 3 : 11.

10 *runs by Salisbury*: the Hampshire Avon.

11 *general*: widely distributed.

CHAPTER 6
Page 77

11 *kipper*: a term applied to the male salmon during the breeding season when the lower jaw becomes hooked upwards.

13 *chaps*: the two bones forming the jaw.

Page 78

2 *Gesner*: see notes to p. 30 above.

24 *in manners*: out of politeness.

Page 79

6 *old Oliver Henly*: cannot be identified.

18 *expression*: the action of pressing or squeezing out.

27 *conclusion*: experiment.

31 *Polypody of the Oak*: a fern which grows on oaks.

35–6 *Sir George Hastings*: see notes to p. 58 above.

Page 80

2 *Tecon*: a northern dialect term for salmon.

CHAPTER 7

Page 81

3 *Gesner*: see notes to p. 30 above.

4 *Pikrell-weed*: pickerel-weed is a name applied to various types of pondweed amongst which pike breed.

18 *chargeable*: burdensome or costly.

28 *It is a hard thing to perswade the belly, . . .*: proverbial. Cf. Tilley, B 286: 'The Belly has no ears.'

Page 82

15–16 *Lake Thracimane*: Lake Trasimeno in central Italy.

Page 83

4 *curiosity*: the disposition to inquire too minutely into anything.

Page 84

25 *Topsell*: see notes to p. 58 above.

26 *Frog-Padock*: toad.

33 *Cardanas*: Girolamo Cardano (1501–76), Italian mathematician, physician and astrologer. The work referred to is his *De Subtilitate Rerum* (1551), where he explains that frogs and fishes sometimes fall as rain after they have been carried off from high places by the wind.

Page 85

1 *right*: true.

4 *simber*: obsolete form of 'simmer'. Refers to salts produced through evaporation.

10–11 *mouth grows up*: refers to the myth, perhaps derived from the fact that frogs hibernate, that frogs' mouths become permanently closed during the winter months.

24 *bow*: bough of a tree.

28 *ravelling*: unravelling.

33 *powch*: swallow.

NOTES

Page 86

14 *bottles of hay*: bundles of hay.
   flags: reeds or rushes.
24 *commute*: to exchange an obligation for something lighter or more agreeable.
26 *Oyle of Spike*: an oil obtained by distillation of french lavender.

Page 87

3 *Margerom*: marjoram.
4 *Winter-Savoury*: small evergreen shrub.
13 *filiting*: thread.
25 *hogoe*: 'hogo' or 'haut-goût' refers to a high flavour.

CHAPTER 8
Page 88

4 *Mr Mascall*: Leonard Mascall (*d.* 1589), translator and author. His *A Booke of Fishing with Hooke and Line* (1590) states that carp were introduced into the country by a 'maister Mascoll of Plumsted in Sussex' who was presumably not a relation, although Mascall himself came from an old Plumstead family.
22 *grass, or flags*: reeds or rushes.

Page 89

9 *watched*: guarded.
25 *considerable*: worth considering.

Page 90

4 *Janus Dubravius*: Johann Dubraw (*d.* 1553), Bishop of Olmütz in modern Czechoslovakia. His *De Piscinis* (1559) was translated as *A New Booke of Good Husbandry* (1599).
23 *remember*: remind.

Page 92

4 *Virgins-wax*: pure wax.
9 *Oyl of Peter ... Oyl of the Rock*: naphtha or petroleum.

CHAPTER 9
Page 93

12 *Docks*: common name for various species of coarse, weedy herbs.
30 *Randelitius*: see notes to p. 30 above.

Page 94

2 *Solomon* (*who knew the nature of all things from the Shrub to the Cedar*): cf. I Kings 4:29–33.

Page 95

7 *Apothecaries*: druggist.
8 *reins*: kidneys.

15 *Sir Abraham Williams*: Sir Abraham Williams (*fl.* 1619) acted as agent in England for the Elector Palatine and Princess Elizabeth of Bohemia.

Page 96

23 *Doctor Donne*: see notes to p. 34 above.

Page 97

1–28 Donne's poem is modelled on Marlowe's 'Come Live with Me', which the milkmaid had earlier sung. Walton's version includes several minor variations from Donne's text.

23 *sleave*: to separate silk thread into its filaments.

CHAPTER 10
Page 98

3 *daintie*: pleasing to the palate.

29 *Bede*: the Venerable Bede (*c.* 673–735), Anglo-Saxon theologian and historian. Gesner quoted Bede's *Ecclesiastical History of the English People* (*c.* 731).

Page 99

2 *Dubartas*: see notes to p. 30 above.

3 *Cambden*: see notes to p. 29 above.

Gerrard: see notes to p. 65 above.

13 *Crassus*: Lucius Licinius Crassus (140–91 B.C.), Roman politician and lawyer famous for his oratory.

23 *Albertus*: see notes to p. 58 above.

30 *curious*: diligent.

Page 100

19 *common*: generally known.

CHAPTER 11
Page 102

3 *wattels*: wattles are the fleshy appendages hanging from the mouths of some fish.

20 *River Danubie*: river Danube.

Page 103

5 *Plutark*: Plutarch (*c.* A.D. 46–*c.* 120), Greek biographer, whose *The Lives of the Noble Grecians and Romanes*, trans. Thomas North (1579), was a standard work.

22–3 *Sheeps tallow*: a substance derived from animal fat, used to make candles.

28 *tryes conclusions*: experiments.

Page 104

14 *lease*: that is, a 'leash', a hunting term for a set of three.

26 *Sillabub*: see notes to p. 36 above.

31 *once in a Month*: visit at monthly intervals.

37 *to enter*: to initiate.

Page 105

2 *hardly*: not easily.

18 *reserved*: secluded.

19 *easie Angler*: easy-going.

27 *answerable*: corresponding.

30 *Sir Henry Wotton*: see notes to p. 17 above.

Page 106

15 *just*: precisely.

26 *shovel-board*: shove-halfpenny.

31 *Ketch*: see notes to p. 53 above.

32 *doged*: ill-tempered.

33 *want*: lack or miss.

Page 107

5 The poem is by Jo. Chalkhill. See notes to p. 53 above.

17 *Aurora*: See notes to p. 37 above.

37 *intangle*: entangle or ensnare.

Page 108

7 *fray*: frighten.

14 *Osier*: a species of willow.

32 *toyes*: trifles.

Page 109

7 *without replications*: without reply or protest.

17 18 *depending*: pending.

24 5 *Lady-smocks*: cuckoo-flower.

25 *Culverkeys*: bluebells.

28 *the field in Sicily*: a reference to Greek mythology. Pluto snatched Persephone from a field in Sicily.

Diodorus: Diodorus Siculus (*fl.* first century B.C.), Greek historian.

30 *sent*: scent.

32 *ought*: owned.

33 4 *the meek possess the earth*: Matthew 5:5.

36 *the Poet*: again cannot be identified, but is possibly Walton himself.

Page 110

12 ff. The accompanying music (see appendix) was written by Henry Lawes (1596–1662), who also provided the music for Milton's *Comus* (1634). The verse comes, with the usual slight variations, from Phineas Fletcher's *The Purple Island* (1633).

27–32 The verse is derived from a poem by 'W.D.' (possibly Sir William Davenant) found in John Hilton's *Catch that Catch Can* (1652).

33–4 *seasonably*: at the right moment.

CHAPTER 12

Page 112

18 *pottle*: a half-gallon.

32 *All-hollantide*: All-Hallows day is 1 November.

Page 113

1 *greenswards*: turf.

10 *peck*: a measure of two gallons.

11 *firkin*: a small cask.

23 *Michaelmas*: the feast of St Michael, 29 September.

24 *Kite*: these birds of prey were formerly common in England.

30 *nice*: unwilling.

Page 114

15 *trencher*: a flat piece of wood on which meat was cut and served.

21 2 *Sir George Hastings*: see notes to p. 58 above.

22 *Sir Henry Wotton*: see notes to p. 17 above.

30 *Rosi-crutions*: the Rosicrucians were supposed members of a secret brotherhood claiming to possess occult wisdom handed down from the ancients.

33 *flote fish*: those caught by float-fishing.

35 6 *sport sake*: for the sake of entertainment.

36 *old Fish-book*: cannot be identified.

Page 115

1 6 The source of this rhyme is unknown.

11 *Dr Nowel*: see notes to p. 34 above.

23 *Totenham High-Cross*: an ancient wooden cross marked the centre of Tottenham.

32 *Frumitie*: frumenty, a dish made of wheat boiled in milk, seasoned with cinnamon, sugar, etc.

Page 116

3 *relate*: to be united to larger rivers. According to the *OED* the usage is unique to Walton.

6 *a two pence*: a small silver coin.

12 *spur*: the back claw.

21 *bents*: grass-like reeds and sedges.

36 *curiosity*: elaborateness or perfection of construction.

CHAPTER 13

Page 118

13 *Allome*: alum, a whitish transparent mineral salt

14 *pipkin*: a small earthenware pot or pan.

16 *hair*: see notes to p. 67 above.

26 *pottle*: see notes to p. 112 above.

30 *Copporis*: copperas, iron sulphate, also known as green vitriol.

32 *wasted*: evaporated.

Page 119

5 *Verdigreece*: verdigris, a green or greenish-blue substance obtained by the action of dilute acetic acid on plates of copper and much used in the process of dyeing.

8–9 *lie colour*: colour of alkalized water, that is, almost colourless.

10 *white lead*: a mixture of lead carbonate and hydrated lead oxide.

11 *red lead*: a red oxide of lead.
     black: graphite.

16 *Pink*: a yellowish or greenish-yellow pigment.

18 *drive*: to spread out thinly.

29 *motion*: proposal.

30 *Sack*: a general name for a class of wine imported from Spain and the Canaries.

34 *Copy printed amongst Sir Henry Wottons Verses* ...: the poem which follows, 'A Description of the Countrey's Recreations', is included in *Reliquiae Wottonianae* (1651), where it is signed 'ignoto'. Walton edited the volume and clearly had doubts concerning the authorship of the poem, for he placed it among the group merely 'found among the papers' of Wotton.

Page 120

8 *fond*: foolish.

9 *glosing*: putting on a specious appearance.

11 *Mummery*: hypocritical play-acting.

29 *Mask*: masque.

Page 121

6 *price*: praise.

14 *Ceres*: the goddess of corn in Latin mythology.

27 *Dr. D.*: John Donne. Walton's attribution of the poem to Donne is supported by a number of manuscript attributions. However, Walton clearly had his doubts and in the third and later editions of *The Compleat Angler* attributed the poem to Wotton.

34 *damask'd*: of the colour of the damask rose; blush-coloured.

Page 122

23 *Minion*: favourite.

24 *Angels*: angels were English gold coins.

27 *by*: buy.

Page 123

19 *Saint Peters Master*: Christ.

MORE ABOUT PENGUINS, PELICANS
AND PUFFINS

For further information about books available from Penguins please write to Dept EP, Penguin Books Ltd, Harmondsworth, Middlesex UB7 0DA.

In the U.S.A.: For a complete list of books available from Penguins in the United States write to Dept DG, Penguin Books, 299 Murray Hill Parkway, East Rutherford, New Jersey 07073.

In Canada: For a complete list of books available from Penguins in Canada write to Penguin Books Canada Ltd, 2801 John Street, Markham, Ontario L3R 1B4.

In Australia: For a complete list of books available from Penguins in Australia write to the Marketing Department, Penguin Books Australia Ltd, P.O Box 257, Ringwood, Victoria 3134.

In New Zealand: For a complete list of books available from Penguins in New Zealand write to the Marketing Department, Penguin Books (N.Z.) Ltd, Private Bag, Takapuna 9, Auckland.

In India: For a complete list of books available from Penguins in India write to Penguin Overseas Ltd, 706 Eros Apartments, 56 Nehru Place, New Delhi 110019.

THE RIVER WHY

David James Duncan

Son of a stuffy and world-famous flyfishing writer and his raucous, bait-fishing, cowgirl wife, Gus Orviston takes refuge in a secluded cabin on the banks of the Tamanawis after a seemingly insoluble dispute over Izaak Walton's *The Compleat Angler*.

There Gus devotes himself to his true love – fishing – under the relentless Ideal Schedule. But bliss eludes him and he becomes increasingly troubled by the degradation of the natural world and the spiritual barrenness of his own life. Embarking on a reluctant quest to the river's source, he encounters such unexpected charaters as Thomas Bigeater, a sage old Indian; Titus, a self-styled philosopher and his wise dog, Descartes; and, most importantly, a beautiful and enigmatic fisherwoman.

The River Why is an exuberant and unforgettable story about the relationships between men, women and their environment, in which we come to share a moving appreciation of the connectedness between all creatures on this watery planet.

THE PENGUIN GUIDE TO FRESHWATER FISHING
IN BRITAIN AND IRELAND

Ted Lamb

An up-to-date, authoritative guide to freshwater fishing for coarse and game anglers.

The British Isles are well blessed with fishing waters of every description, from the lush Southern English watermeadows to the tumbling rivers of the uplands, from quiet carp pools to huge reservoirs and the die-straight drains under the broad skies of the Somerset and East Anglian flatlands.

Whatever the location, freshwater fishing is bound by rules, and Ted Lamb's invaluable book with provide you with all the necessary information about rod licences, fishing rights and regulations, and how to apply for fishing permission, as well as with the names of angling organizations.

This freshwater guide and gazetteer for game and coarse anglers complements *The Penguin Guide to Sea Fishing in Britain and Ireland*.

FISH COOKERY

Jane Grigson

There are over fifty species of edible fish, and Jane Grigson feels that most of us do not eat nearly enough of them.

If anything will make us mend our ways, it is this delightful book with its varied and comprehensive recipes, covering everything from lobster to conger eel, from sole to clam chowder. Many of her dishes come from France, others are from the British Isles, America, Spain, Italy – any country where good fish is cooked with loving care and eaten with appreciation.

'More than a book of recipes, there's precise information on all aspects of fish cookery; stories and legends connected with fish as well as all the practical information needed to buy, clean, cook, preserve and cure fish' – *Lady*

'One of the three most influential and popular cookery writers in Britain' – *The Times*

'Like Elizabeth David, she writes like an angel' – *Sunday Times*

THE FLOUNDER

Günter Grass

Günter Grass, says *The Times*, 'is on his own as an artist'. And indeed this extraordinary, provoking and joyously Rabelaisian celebration of life, food and sex is unique.

Lifted from their ancient fairytale, the fisherman and his wife are still living today. During the months of Ilsebill's pregnancy the fisherman tells her of his adventures through time with the Flounder, whose magic powers have been responsible for male predominance. What has happened to him, to the cooks of each age and to the Flounder, eventually faced with the anger of a feminist tribunal, constitutes a complete reworking of social, political and gastronomic history.

The Flounder is a rich and many-layered novel, redolent with good food, laced with poetry and spiced with wit and humour. Enormously enjoyable, it is 'the novel of a man at the height of remarkable powers'.

'Imaginative, witty ... he is a man of extraordinary talents' – *Spectator*

MOBY-DICK

Herman Melville
Edited by Harold Beaver

'It is of the horrible texture of a fabric that should be woven of ships' cables and hawsers. A Polar wind blows through it, and birds of prey hover over it.'

So Melville about his masterpiece; and into his tale of Captain Ahab's insane quest of the white whale he poured all of his own youthful experience and a minute study of the literature of whales and whaling; but into it also went other experiences, other reading, other insights ... into the 'power of blackness' and the deepest dreams and obsessions of mankind.

For the splendours of *Moby-Dick* are complex, a rich mixture of sea-time and book-learning, full of allusion, parody, pun and verbal echo, the kind of learned playfulness we associate with Joyce and Nabokov and Borges. In the intestines of this 'whale of a book' lie the seeds of the modernist movement.

For this edition Harold Beaver has supplied a lengthy commentary to guide the reader through the labyrinth of *Moby-Dick* to a deeper understanding of its mysteries.

PENGUIN TRAVEL BOOKS

☐ *A Time of Gifts* **Patrick Leigh Fermor** £2.95

In 1933 the author set out to walk to Constantinople. This award-winning book carries him as far as Hungary and is, to Philip Toynbee, 'more than just a Super-travel-book' and, according to Jan Morris, 'a masterpiece'.

☐ *A Reed Shaken by the Wind* **Gavin Maxwell** £2.95

Staying in reed houses on tiny man-made islands, Maxwell journeyed through the strange, unexplored marshlands of Iraq. His unusual book is 'a delight' – *Observer*

☐ *Third-Class Ticket* **Heather Wood** £3.95

A rich landowner left enough money for forty Bengali villagers to set off, third-class, and 'see all of India'. This wonderful account is 'wholly original, fantastic, but true' – *Daily Telegraph*

☐ *Slow Boats to China* **Gavin Young** £3.50

On an ancient steamer, a cargo dhow, a Filipino kumpit and twenty more agreeably cranky boats, Young sailed from Piraeus to Canton in seven crowded and colourful months. 'A pleasure to read' – Paul Theroux

☐ *Granite Island* **Dorothy Carrington** £3.95

The award-winning portrait of Corsica that magnificently evokes the granite villages, the beautiful mountains and olive trees as well as the history, beliefs, culture and personality of its highly individualistic island people.

☐ *Venture to the Interior* **Laurens van der Post** £2.95

A trek on foot through the breathtaking scenery and secret places of Central Africa, described by one of the great explorers and travellers of our time.

PENGUIN TRAVEL BOOKS

☐ *Brazilian Adventure* **Peter Fleming** £2.95

'. . . To explore rivers Central Brazil, if possible ascertain fate Colonel Fawcett . . .' – this is the exciting account of what happened when Fleming answered this advertisement in *The Times*.

☐ *Mani* **Patrick Leigh Fermor** £2.95

Part travelogue, part inspired evocation of the people and culture of the Greek Peloponnese, this is 'the masterpiece of a traveller and scholar' – *Illustrated London News*

☐ *As I Walked Out One Midsummer Morning*
Laurie Lee £1.95

How he tramped from the Cotswolds to London, and on to Spain just before the Civil War, recalled with a young man's vision and exuberance. 'A beautiful piece of writing' – *Observer*

☐ *The Light Garden of the Angel King* **Peter Levi** £2.95

Afghanistan has been a wild rocky highway for nomads and merchants, Alexander the Great, Buddhist monks, great Moghul conquerors and the armies of the Raj. Here, brilliantly, Levi discusses their journeys and his own.

☐ *The Worst Journey in the World*
Apsley Cherry-Garrard £5.95

An account of Scott's last Antarctic Expedition, 1910–13. 'It is – what few travellers' tales are – absolutely and convincingly credible' – George Bernard Shaw

☐ *The Old Patagonian Express* **Paul Theroux** £2.50

From blizzard-stricken Boston down through South America, railroading by luxury express and squalid local trains, to Argentina – a journey of vivid contrasts described in 'one of the most entrancing travel books' – C. P. Snow

PENGUIN TRAVEL BOOKS

☐ *Hindoo Holiday* J. R. Ackerley   £2.95

Ackerley's journal of his career as companion to the Maharajah of Chhokrapur in the twenties. 'Radiantly delightful . . . A book difficult to praise . . . temperately' – Evelyn Waugh

☐ *The Marsh Arabs* Wilfred Thesiger   £2.95

'This voyage through desert waters will remain, like his *Arabian Sands*, a classic of travel writing' – *The Times*

☐ *A Pattern of Islands* Arthur Grimble   £2.95

Full of gleaming humour and anecdotes, this is the true story (and a popular classic) of an Englishman living among the fishermen, sorcerers, fighters and poets of the Pacific islands.

These books should be available at all good bookshops or news-agents, but if you live in the UK or the Republic of Ireland and have difficulty in getting to a bookshop, they can be ordered by post. Please indicate the titles required and fill in the form below.

NAME _____ BLOCK CAPITALS

ADDRESS _____

_____

_____

Enclose a cheque or postal order payable to The Penguin Bookshop to cover the total price of books ordered, plus 50p for postage. Readers in the Republic of Ireland should send £IR equivalent to the sterling prices, plus 67p for postage. Send to: The Penguin Bookshop, 54/56 Bridlesmith Gate, Nottingham, NG1 2GP.

You can also order by phoning (0602) 599295, and quoting your Barclaycard or Access number.

Every effort is made to ensure the accuracy of the price and availability of books at the time of going to press, but it is sometimes necessary to increase prices and in these circumstances retail prices may be shown on the covers of books which may differ from the prices shown in this list or elsewhere. This list is not an offer to supply any book.

This order service is only available to residents in the UK and the Republic of Ireland.